Old Wine, Late Bloom

My Take on Selected Issues

Eugenio A. Pulmano, MD
2014

Old Wine, Late Bloom

Self-published & printed in USA by Tatay Jobo Elizes with Author's permission using Print-On-Demand System (POD) and Kindle Edition. Tatay Jobo Elizes is a Self-Publisher in USA. Published in 2012 under the following ISBN numbers.

ISBN-13 - 978: 1500890513
ISBN-10: 1500890510

Eugenio A. Pulmano, MD   2

About the Author

Dr. Eugene A. Pulmano finished his medical degree from University of the Philippines in 1969 and practice medicine as an internist in the State of New Jersey, until he retired recently.

Dedication

This book is dedicated to the Filipino people

Contents

Introduction
(By Tatay Jobo Elizes, Self-Publisher)

Writings need to be recorded as they act as mirrors of history. You don't have to be a good writer to write something. The only requirement is to write in simple terms to be understood. I have seen a lot of good writings in the internet, in magazines and newspapers. But most writers have only one or two articles and therefore not enough material to be published as a book. And yet, many of them need to be published.

I am offering these services free of charge because of the availability of print-books-on-demand (POD) system nowadays. I have acquired the knowledge the hard way. I am now in a position to help publish writings of anybody. I assume the initial cost, but the final books are for sale at a famous online store at very affordable prices.. Prints are always available ex-stock and never run out of prints. You don't need to reprint, forever.

Why put your writings in a book? And not just in the internet? I recommend that writings be retained in a hard copy or in book form or printed form for posterity. The book will always be there among your collections or libraries. Not all use the internet. The internet access has its technical problems. Writings in the internet may be erased erroneously. Free storage is hard to access. Paid storage may be returned or lost.

For those looking for a publisher, especially if you have a novel or many essays, I can produce the paperback book under your own authorship. Book sale is risky business. In most cases, I cannot even recover my initial costs. As authors, you must help in marketing these books that contain your writings.

Book is a matter of pride, for the author. It took me a couple of years to convince Dr. Eugenio A. Pulmano to publish his own book. He happens to be articulate and up-to-date on world events and issues. Please critique this book if you have the time. Happy reading!

Eugenio A. Pulmano, MD   *5*

1
The Filipino Identity and
The Filipino Dream

Dateline: 2014

Last week I went to see my doctor in the Jersey City, where I used to practice, for a scheduled nerve conduction studies and electromyogram (EMG). He is a physiatrist, a doctor of medicine specializing in physical and rehabilitation medicine. I used to refer most of my patients to him, because he was/is the best in Hudson County, if not in the entire state of NJ; he would take his time doing a procedure, meticulous in evaluating patients, and his feedback report had always been a pleasure to read.

Anyway, as my physiatrist was doing my NCS and EMG, we came to talk about many other things. He mentioned his missionary work in India and his touring of Asian countries but the Philippines. He wished he had visited the country, because as it turned out later, he ended up in Jersey City where many of his patients are Filipinos. Jersey City has a large population of *Pinoys*. He regretted the fact that he knows so little of the Filipino people and the Philippines. He knows vaguely about the Battle of Manila Bay. I had to fill in gaps in his knowledge about that battle. I had to impress on him that that famous (infamous) battle was a sham; before that battle the fate of the Philippine was already foreordained at the Treaty of Paris, at which the Philippines was ceded (sold) by the Spain to America for the sum of $ 20 M. Under the pretext of liberating us, America chose to stay and occupy us for geopolitical and trade and commercial reasons. I could have added a few more details to this historical event, but did not want him to get distracted from the procedure he was doing on me.

But before we left the topic of the Philippines and Filipinos, though, he asked me a tough question, out of a sincere desire to know more about us. He asked: "Can you tell me something of the Filipino identity?" I suppose in spite of his many contacts with Filipino patients and other professionals like doctors and nurses in the health field, he probably could not put his finger on who are the Filipinos, in contradistinction with the ease with which the Chinese, Koreas, Japanese and Indians, who come more or less come from same geographic part of the world, are known. He could not have asked me a more difficult question, about which our writers, historians and intellectuals have a hard themselves to define. Caught somewhat off-guard, I groped for an answer, and fell back on Nick Joaquin's response faced with a similar question: "The Filipino identity is in the process of becoming," and gave him the barest outline of our history and culture in almost a power point-presentation from the time the ten datus from the Malay-Indonesian region arrived in our shores, to and through the Spanish regime, to the American interlude including the Commonwealth period, WW II and the Japanese occupation, to the granting of our independence in 1946, post WWII the reconstruction period and more recent history, e.g. waves of immigration to the US and other parts of the world.

For sure this was a sprint through our history and culture. I don't know if my friend made any sense out of it, got a better idea of what and who we are.

Given more time or more occasions with him, I would have fleshed out the high and low points of our history and culture and walked him more leisurely through our narrative, if only for him to have a better idea and appreciation of us as a people. It would have gone this way:

Pre-Spanish Time

Our standard and conventional history started with ten datus that sailed from the Malaysian-Indonesian region and landed, more like stumbled, and settled upon the many islands that constitute the country we now call the Philippines.

They found the islands congenial to good living; nature was kind to them. The land was richly endowed with all they needed. The soil was fertile; rainfall was more than sufficient. You stick a plant's twig and in no time would yield bountiful leaves, stems, fruits or vegetables. In the mountains, rolling hills and flat lands plenty of various hardy trees grew like Molave, Yakal, Mahogany, Narra, all excellent for building their houses and their banca. Trees of santol, bayabas, langka, mangga, atis, lumboy, chico, etc. generously yielded with their fruits, all for the taking by anybody in the village. Rivers and lakes crisscrossed the land, yielding a good variety of fish in abundance. The people traveled from one place to another via these waterways. Games of wild pigs, wild chickens and birds were aplenty in the mountains and in the hills. The weather was typically warm, but very much tolerable. The air that they breathe was wholesome. Generally men and women wore all-weather clothes. Women wore skirt, and some I imagine were topless; that was the age of innocence; there was no malice. Men were very comfortable and not self-conscious at all with their g-strings; they were mostly shirtless. Few put on t-shirts. Festivities were not unknown to them; dishes consisting of boiled fish seasoned with spices and herbs mixed with vegetables, broiled fish, grilled boar, and native delicacies were served wrapped in banana leaves. Alcoholic beverages like tuba, basi or lambanog would enliven gatherings. Tales of adventure by young and old would be told and retold. Celebrations would not be complete without singing and dancing. Life was good and idyllic in the islands; life's rhythms were dictated by the seasons, by the movement of the moon and the stars.

Now and then the townspeople would paddle their boats through rivers and lakes to visit kin and friends in other villages; sometimes they'd put on sails to travel to other island to barter for some goods or to meet rulers of other tribes.

The different tribes were at peace with one another for the most part, each tribe largely autonomous, for life was good in their own corners of the world. There was no need to invade and subdue other tribes, to covet their land or their women. Occasionally, maybe, there would be some frictions between tribes, maybe some skirmishes, but certainly not war to conquer other tribes. Sooner or later, these altercations would be resolved by the village elders and wound up with happy celebrations; eating, drinking and dancing marked those occasions.

Although they were autonomous--because to start with they all came from the same ethno-linguistic groups and regions in Southwest Asia--there was an underlying common denominator of language and cultural traits that would bind each to the other. Because of some geographical distances from each other and blissfully self-sufficient and generally at peace with one another, their social-political and economic relationships were both relaxed and loose, not by defined by rigid norms and criteria that characterize what we'd call today a country, much less a nation. At once at peace with one another and with nature, the Indios live in the "Garden of Eden," sort of.

The Spanish Time

Then out the deep blue sea (Pacific Ocean) appeared the first colonizers, the Spaniards, bearing the Sword and the Cross. They ostensibly came in peace and in search of the highly valued spices of the East, first made known to the West by Marco Polo. Initially they were welcomed by our people. It soon became apparent, however, what their true motives were: To subjugate our people and possess their land. Our people saw through this. At Mactan Island, Ferdinand Magellan, credited by historians to be the first man to have circumnavigated the world, fell before the spears of Lapu-Lapu. But the invaders were nothing but persistent. Spain sent a number of expeditions to our "Garden of Eden." Finally, under the commandership of Legaspi, they gained a foothold in Cebu. He soon moved his forces to Manila, which became his command post and seat of government. From there he launched expeditions and attacks to other islands and tribes. Because our people were not one nation, one country, and backed by superior weapons Legaspi found it easy to conquer one tribe after another. Very soon they lorded over the entire land except for Mindanao, the biggest island in the south where the Muslims centuries earlier, ca. 1300, established their kingdom.

It was if our people were driven from "Paradise." They were not only internally exiled but made to be slaves in their own land. The conquerors were supposed to have come with the Sword and the Cross. In reality it was mostly by the sword that they subdued the natives. And for those who were supposed to announce, and bear witness to, the Good News, many of them acted as if they too wielded the sword more than the cross; they behaved no better; instead of looking for the spiritual welfare of the Indios they were as worldly as the civilian authorities; they forgot their primary duty to save the natives' souls for life hereafter; for some the lure of the flesh did not escape them; they impregnated our women and some kept them in the convent, to shield their misdeeds and sins.

To the victor belonged the spoil. They took possession of the land; large tracts of land were distributed to their officer-soldiers as rewards for their exploits in the form of haciendas and econmiendas, some were given to the religious orders. Of course, those lands needed to be cleared and cultivated; who else but our people did the heavy pulling? Forced labor was imposed. On top of which taxes were exacted on them; this dirty job was delegated to the chosen collectors, given a small percentage of what they collected as incentives, which became little source of corruption. For the land they grabbed, they recruited overseers, who received some material incentives too. The children of these chosen few accumulated some money and materials assets and were able to send their schools in Manila; for even fewer numbers their sons traveled and studied in Europe, primarily in Spain. Our national hero, Jose Rizal, Luna brothers, Hidalgo, Marcelo H. Del Pilar, among others, were the lucky ones who traveled and studied in Spain.

Education though was a dangerous thing. It was the Age of Enlightenment and the Industrial Revolution. The Indios were susceptible to, and absorbed readily, the progressive ideas then in circulation in Europe. They formed a "Propaganda Movement" that pointed to the abuses back home, wrote about the new ideas learned. It was in Europe that Rizal wrote his "Noli" and "Fili," which found its way eventually to the homeland, struck a chord among the Indios, not only from the educated few, but from the common people by word of mouth. When our writers and intellectuals returned back home, they found the conditions even worse; they were struck by the stark contrast between what they learned in Europe and what they saw in the homeland: injustices and abuses by the civilian and secular authorities. They agitated for reforms. They only reaped reprisals; they were punished in variety of ways: jailed and dispossessed of their land and other possessions. Some were executed. Fathers Gomez, Burgos and Zamora come readily to mind.

The land of peace and abundance was no more. Discord and disorder came over the land. The natives were pitted against each other. Some of them, for their own interest, easily sided with their conquerors and became their tools. For this they were richly rewarded. They were given enough to have a semblance of the life of their masters; some of them, in fact, looked down upon their people, if not accomplices in the enslavement of their own people.

Three hundred years of Spanish regime...we cannot help but imbibed their culture. Take the fiesta for instance which we have taken to heart and elevated it to excessive heights. I was in med school when one of my dorm mates, who came from a Southern town in Luzon, invited me to their hometown fiesta. It was my first time to attend a fiesta in another province. I was quite surprised that along the main street in the plaza you could go to any house, as long as you tag along with somebody who knew somebody in the house or home, and partake of the food prepared. The table literally was laden with dishes of all kinds. My friend and I must have gone to four houses, engorged ourselves with food. I could just imagine how much each home spent for the lavish preparations: food plus the ostentatious decorations. I bet you a number of homeowners who got into some debt simply to put on an impressive reception for their guests. (Because of the hard times these days, this practice has been muted, in contrast to the "roaring 50s and 60s.")

And then you have such quasi-religious celebrations such as Santa Cruzan or Flores de Mayo, devoid for the most part of religious content, but have become events of spectacle, pomp and circumstances. You have "Hermano Mayor" and "Hermana Mayor" who are asked to be the main sponsors for the celebration; they practically feed the whole townspeople; some these sponsors probably spend far more than they can really afford. When I was young, of course, I loved to watch these parades or processions, because you would normally see the most beautiful ladies, celebrities, show biz people in the town. These occasions had come to be events "to see and be seen." I don't know why the church tolerated or encouraged such conspicuous show and consumption. I could understand the underlying religious roots of these events, sort of manifestation of religious piety, but they have become so excessive that the religious significance has been virtually lost. This public display of excesses was/is emblematic of the misguided aspirations of the Filipinos for the "good life" that they were witnesses to, indulged in by the elites during their 300 years of Spanish colonization.

This public display of piety and religiosity was obscenely juxtaposed with many public officials' looting of public coffers and other corrupt practices. The late Fr. Bulatao, the renowned Jesuit psychologist, referred to this as "Split Christianity."

During the Spanish times, it was not uncommon for the Indios to be under "double jeopardy." There was hardly any separation of church and civilian authorities; many times they were in collusion in abusing the Indios. Rizal and many of our writer-heroes wrote extensively about such abuses. Rizal's novels "Noli Me Tangere" & "El Filibusterismo" depict many instances of Spanish oppression and abuses.

In the meantime, many natives lost their nerves, their self-esteem, looked down upon themselves; they coveted the affluent lifestyle of their new masters. They looked up to them, aspired to live or envied the life of their masters. Most became totally dependent on their masters. The abundance that was once theirs was gone, appropriated by conquerors.

The oppression of the poor Indios continued. Those who had had the benefit of education, who initially tried to clamor for reform, for justice, saw their efforts useless and invited only retaliations. Rizal's family was   the recipients of such abuses and retribution. Under such circumstances it did not take long before the idea of complete independence dawned on them. Peaceful means had been tried, to no avail, bringing only more of the same abuses and griefs. Rebellion was seen as the only viable option. Yet, there was a great deal of equivocation among our heroes. Rizal was basically for reform and was said to be reluctant to endorse the revolution against Spain, arguing that the people were not ready for such a drastic and bloody upheaval.

The Rise of the Indios.

Ready or not, Andres Bonifacio, who came from humble circumstances and did not have a sentimental love for Spain and Spanish culture and saw only the dark side of Spanish regime, lit the fuse of rebellion. Rebellion spread to many regions in the country, although there was minimal coordination. Internal struggles within the Katipunan leadership between Bonifacio and Aguinaldo ensued. Aguinaldo prevailed. The fight continued on under him. There were no shortage of recruits to the cause, but firearms and ammunitions were short supply. Some of our revolutionary leaders were dispatched to Hong Kong or Japan to enlist some help or buy some firearms.

There was an interesting episode here. About that time, China under the leadership of Dr. Sun Yat Sen and his fellow nationalists, were waging a nationalist rebellion of their own against the oppressive and corrupt regime of then Chinese Emperor. Many of Dr. Sun Yat Sen's supporters were based in Japan or Hong Kong. There was initial contact between the Philippine revolutionary leaders and top men of Sun Yat Sen. Sun Yet Sen himself was predisposed to supporting the Philippine revolution and pledged to supply arms to our rebels. But on the fateful day of the meeting between Sun Yat Sen and our leaders, the former could not make it; he was under severe attack by the Chinese Emperor's forces. The final negotiations did not take place. Later on Gen. Aguinaldo himself went to Hong Kong to gain support for the rebellion from another emerging world power. He met with Admiral Dewey of the US Navy command; the latter pledged support and set sail toward the Philippines.

In the meantime, despite the rift in the leadership of the *Katipunan*, lack of firearms and other war supplies, the rebels were making progress. Just when they were about to drive out the Spaniards into the Manila Bay, and the Spaniards ready to jump into the Bay and swim into the vast China Sea to drown, lo and behold the Americans led by Dewey steamed into the Manila Bay, ostensibly to liberate us. Aguinaldo was with the liberating forces, quite naïve about what was going on behind his back and around the world. Unbeknown to him and to most of our leaders, a deal had been struck by Spain and America, ceding the Philippines to America for $ 20 M, in the Treaty of Paris. Nonetheless, the "Battle of Manila Bay" was fought. It was nothing but a show. Under the pretext of liberating, civilizing and Christianizing us the Americans stayed.

America & the Manifest Destiny & the White Man's Burden: Civilize & Christianize?

There were some Americans who fought for our independence. Mark Twain, the famed American author, was at the forefront of the Anti-Imperialist League of America. In the chambers of Congress somebody read the Rizal's My Last Farewell, the English translation of Rizal's "Mi Ultimo Adios." At the end of his recitation, he asked his audience, "Are these the people we're supposed to civilize and Christianize?" The silence was deafening.

The Philippine-American War or Philippine Insurrection.

Anyway, for the second time, the Indios mounted a second rebellion from 1898 to 2001 against America, which pestered on for several years more. Our colonizers did not want to label it rebellion or war. It was called the "Philippine Insurrection," suggesting that the uprising was not a legitimate rebellion or war but simply sort of banditry on the part of the Indios; it's not even acknowledged as guerilla warfare. In the course of that conflict atrocities were committed by our occupiers too painful to recall; many decades later such atrocities were committed in another war in mainland Asia. War is hell.

"The American Interlude"

The Americans prevailed, the natives finally pacified. The American administration of the Philippines was benign compared to the Spanish regime. They established a system of public education, giving access to education for most Filipinos; some bright and promising Filipinos were sent to the best schools in America as *pensionados* (scholars). They built hospitals; established public health system, civil service system, the University of the Philippines, which today is the best institution of higher learning in the country; built infrastructures such as roads, bridges and ports.

Cultural Life.

A colony absorbs more than the formal institutions of the colonizer. The various facets of their culture were absorbed through osmosis by the people. These were as effective if not more so as the formal structures in winning the hearts of the people. These included: movies, cigarettes, goods such as chocolates, hot dogs, cookies, clothes, informal gatherings and interactions with people , and...the value of time. The Filipinos enthusiastically imbibed all this but the value of time; they were/still are impervious to this; to this day Filipinos are famous or infamous for being late in almost all informal or for occasions, business meetings or appointments. This cultural flaw appears to be of Spanish influence; a higher social standing seemed to be accorded for those who arrived late; a "dramatic entrance" would catch everybody's attention.

There appeared to be less rigid interaction of classes of people in social gatherings and in more formal occasions. American Big Band music such as jazz, swing, etc. permeated the social scene especially in the capital city, Manila. Hollywood movies, silent and later the talking pictures, became a popular entertainment for Filipinos; later in the post-world war period, this gave rise to the local film industry. American sports like basketball, baseball, track and field came to be loved by Filipinos. "Nightlife" came to be part of social life in Manila among the elites.

Power Structure.

America did not touch the existing power structure in the Philippines. The landed gentry of the Spanish times kept their lands and their socio-economic status. They served as the go-between for Americans with the natives, sort of surrogates, and buffers. The religious orders kept their land. The question of land ownership was at the heart of the agrarian problem from the Spanish times to the American occupation, which persists and pesters to these days, more than 100 years after the beginning of the US occupation of the Philippines, more than half-century after the granting of our independence. These privileges extended to the trade and commerce and politics.

Commonwealth Period.

The Indios, now called Filipinos--divided as they were by ethno-linguistic differences, social and economic status, geography, and influences by American institutions and American ways-- still hungered and agitated for independence. The penultimate outcome of these efforts was the establishment of the Commonwealth status of the Philippines as preparation for a promised independence ten year hence. Under this arrangement a Constitution was drafted under the leadership of the towering intellectual, writer, orator and nationalist Claro M. Recto. The Constitution established a representative democratic government that closely resembled the US, with tripartite bodies, namely, executive, legislative and judiciary. It stipulated the election of a president, vice president; two-chamber legislative body, the Senate and House of Representatives, with the senators elected nationally and the House of Representatives provincially. The president appointed the justices, including the Chief Justice, of the Supreme Court. The judiciary did not adopt the jury system; judges made the decisions and judgments alone. Several levels of appeals court all the way to the SC were provided.

Trade & Commerce:

From the time the Philippines came under the control of the US, there had been trade and commerce between the two countries. The Philippines exported raw and mineral products (e.g., abaca, copra, tobacco, gold, silver,), and in turn, imported finished goods from the US, which Filipinos came to love and still love, getting them relatively cheap because of free trade agreements and overvalued pesos. The upper middle class Filipinos lived like Americans or European with easy access to foreign goods, mostly coming from America. The Filipinos valued American goods, in fact, sort of addicted to them, serving as status symbols, signs of the good life, not realizing the overall cost to the national economy. "Stateside goods" were a "hit" across the spectrum of Philippine society, but a disincentive to building up the Philippine economy.

The trade and commerce became formalized in trade agreements (Bell Trade Act of 1946 superseded by Laurel-Langley Agreement of 1955) whereby sugar quotas were set, the peso pegged to the dollar, repatriation of dollar earnings to the US unhindered, and most important of all, parity rights granted to the Americans in all aspects of trade and commerce, including the exploration and exploitation of our natural resources. Products flowed between the two nations with minimal tariff; later on progressive tariff and more quotas were imposed on Philippine products entering the US.

Security & Military Alliances.

It needs stressing that one of the main reasons for the US occupying the country was to secure a forward placement of its armed forces. It foresaw the growing threat not only posed by Japan but also by China; the other major reason was the US was eyeing the potential huge market for US goods in Asia including Japan and China; the Philippines could be a convenient stepping stone for such commercial purposes. The security and military arrangement, along with trade and commerce between the two countries and cultural exchange, bound the two nations closer together, a relationship dubbed "special relations."

The security arrangements were embodied in the Mutual Defense Act, whereby the US forces leased for 99 years various bases in the Philippines, including the Naval Base in Olongapo/Subic Bay, Sangley Point Naval Base in Cavite, Clark Airbase in Pampanga, Poro Point communications center in La Union, Camp John Hay in Baguio, the summer capital of the Philippines. Under this agreement, an attack on either country by an outside power was taken to mean an attack on the other, and thus each was obligated to come to the aid of the other. One contentious provisions of this agreement, apart from the long duration of the lease of the bases, was that crimes committed by US personnel outside the US bases would be under the jurisdiction of the US government; almost invariably when an American personnel committed a crime in Philippine territory, the Philippines would hand him over to the US government and in always all cases such military personnel was squirreled out of the country. Another point of contention was an attack on the Philippines by a foreign power did not trigger an automatic military response of the US, in contradistinction to US agreement with the NATO nations. Senator Claro M. Recto, a staunch nationalist, vehemently objected to this discriminatory provision of the agreement.

WWII & Its aftermath

Old Wine, Late Bloom

Japanese Occupation. But as fate would have it, there was an abrupt turn in the road to independence. WWII broke and the Philippines was right at the center of it in the Pacific. The Japanese invaded the Philippines, pushed out the Americans and occupied the country. They imposed their will, their way of life and committed various atrocities against civilian populations. They put up a puppet government, and some years later after the war this became a bone of contention, that is, on how to treat those who collaborated with the Japanese. This fight was carried into the political arena after the war; this needlessly polarized the country at the most inopportune time, when it was trying to rise from the ashes of WWII.

The timetable for independence was thus derailed and postponed until after the war, at which time the US was just too eager to grant us independence, ready or not, for both parties. The Americans saddled with the cost of war and peace, that is, reconstruction of Europe embodied in the Marshall Plan and rehabilitation of Japan, was not in a position of rebuilding and running the country. For their part the Filipinos were just as eager to have independence, a fulfillment of their cherished dreams from way back during the Spanish regime.

"I shall I Return."

Gen. Douglas McArthur returned as he promised, and got rid of the Japanese, pursuing them up to their own homeland. But the battle for the liberation of Manila and the country was fierce and exacted a tremendous toll on the country; Manila was reduced to a rubble, the second most devastated city in WWII (Warsaw, Poland was number one, if memory serves). Though independence was finally won, the Philippines laid prostrate. The economy was in ruins. Political life was in turmoil and a ferocious struggle for political supremacy between and among the contending parties; corruption and horse trading in politics were not unknown even then. War reparations from US (mainly) and from Japan did come to the country, they were not nearly enough to rehabilitate the country. Besides, some if not much of the reparations money found its way to the pockets of the politicians and elites of the country.

The trade relations between the Philippines and the US remained the same, the Philippines supplying raw material and minerals, and the Philippines primarily a market for US goods. The agrarian problem persisted and pestered, adding to the political instability of the Philippe for many years; land reform had been time and again emasculated by the powers that be, mostly by the landed gentry. In the meantime, the economic situation of the Philippines was dire.

Industrialization:

Early on there was talk of industrialization, but America decided that the Philippines was not to be the center of industrialization in Asia but Japan; the Philippines had to remain supplier of raw materials and extractive products; agriculture was to be the cornerstone of our economic life (Salvador Araneta, PhD, Dodd's Report and a US Presidential body decision). We were independent and yet not independent, a typical client state, not able to chart her own destiny.

Filipino first Policy.

Notwithstanding all the colonial baggage and the destruction, confusion in the post WWII period and constraints on us, the Filipinos undertook to lift up the economic and social wellbeing of the nation. It embarked on industrialization under Pres. Carlos P. Garcia. For a while it looked promising, light and medium industries were sprouting. It was basically "import substitution," an inward-looking strategy, lacking a wider vision, that is, engaging in world trade. Moreover, our entrepreneurs and businessmen hid under the protectionist policies of the government; they failed to innovate; they got spoiled. The government failed to incentivize them to be more productive, innovative and competitive by imposing a surcharge to their products. Moreover, the exchange control and import control set by the government fell prey to corrupt practices.

Old Wine, Late Bloom

The government's more assertive economic policy, under pressure from international financial multilateral institutions, was upended. The exchange and import controls were dismantled, and the burgeoning industrialization collapsed. This happened under the watch of Pres. Diosdado Macapagal who succeeded Pres. Garcia.

But that's not the hardest blow to the Philippine socio-political-economic life. At the ascension of Marcos as president in 1970, initially the Philippines seemed poised to take off economically. But soon it became evident that Marcos had other things in mind. He made himself a dictator and put in place his cronies in all aspects of Filipino life. Between him and his cronies they looted the coffers of the government. A nuclear power plant in Bataan cost the government around $ 2.2 B, a cost overrun of about $ 1 B; Imelda, the first Lady, raided the Central Bank of the Philippines of tens of millions of dollar. It's recently reported that the offshore accounts of Marcos & family amount to $ 5-10 B that included gold assets amounting to 6.3 metric tons. Nearly all industries and business were under the control of Marcos cronies. Marcos packed all branches of government with his people: judiciary, military and congress. In short, Marcos destroyed all democratic institutions in the country. When he was forced out of office, the Philippine government was left holding the bag with a debt of around $ 70-80 B.

The return of Benigno Aquino from his exile in the US and his assassination at the airport upon his arrival threw the Philippines into turmoil. "People Power" was launched and mobilized, a special election was held, Marcos was defeated, and he and his family and some of his cronies were driven into exile in Hawaii. Corazon Aquino, wife of Benigno Aquino, was elected president. She restored some democratic practices, but she proved to be a weak president and not equal to the task of governance. The old oligarchs and elites, kicked out during the Marcos regime, quickly exacted their vengeance and in no time took back what they lost under Marcos and more.

Subsequent leaders did not perform any better. Pres. Ramos, at first looked promising but in the end left the government coffers empty; Pres. Estrada who followed Ramos got indicted and convicted of plunder. Pres. Gloria Macapagal-Arroyo (GMA) who ousted Pres. Estrada proved to be another Marcos if not worse. She is presently indicted for plunder.

Pres. Benigno Aquino III was elected president after the term of GMA ; he's now in his third year, and there seems to be faint signs of improvement and hope. In his first two years of office, he was able to have Chief Justice of the Supreme Court impeached. At the recently concluded national elections and local elections, most of his candidates won. It remains to be seen if he can consolidate his power and put in place the important changes in the government that can be more responsive to the challenges facing the nation. The 2013 election o appeared to be marred by a good deal of cheating and anomalies. Dynasties dominated the senatorial race; they did so also for many of the provincial races for governors and congressmen.

In the meantime, because of the weakened economy from the time of Marcos regime and exploding population, tens of thousands of Filipinos have chosen to go abroad for employment, accepting menial jobs to support their families, sometimes at extreme risks to their lives and limbs, in a manner of "kapit sa patalim." That's how desperate some Filipinos are. You cannot blame them; if they stay, they die of hunger or from ever lurking diseases.

The above is sprint through and an overview of our history and cultural heritage from the pre-Hispanic times to the present.

NOT YET CONCEIVED AS A NATION, ITs POTENTIAL COMPONENT PARTS WERE ALREAD DISMEMBERED.

The thing to note here is that before the Spaniards came we were not one nation; we were "many nations," more like tribes or fiefdoms, each largely autonomous, and at peace with themselves and one another. There was no impetus for one tribe to dominate another or for one ruler to consolidate all the fiefdoms under his rule. There was no need. Life was good for everyone. Though all came from the same geographic region in the South West Asia, there was no robust shared cultural traits that bound them to make one nation. The ten datus who came to our shores apparently were part of loose empire in the South West Asia and they were possibly at the periphery of it; this contributed to their lack of cohesion or integration culturally or otherwise. And when they immigrated to our shores whatever cultural ties or alliances they had, in time, in the various islands they settled in, that minimum of shared culture got even more diluted and possibly weakened because of geographic factors, posing difficulties in inter-tribal interaction. Certainly, there was nobody ambitious enough or aggressive enough to lord it over the other tribes to establish a kingdom that could even be remotely called a country much less a nation. There was hardly a "collective unconscious" or "collective consciousness" that would bind them together for common defensive purposes or adventurism for conquest, or at the very least, for constructive enterprises that would benefit all the tribes.

This proved to be a great disadvantage when confronted by the succession of colonizers that arrived in our shores. They could not present a common front; they were unprepared for such a scenario. Thus they easily fell prey to the determined objective of conquest by their colonizers with their superior firepower and to the all too common tactics of colonizers to divide and rule, pitting one tribe against another.

Long after the colonizers were gone, with the havoc brought on the land by them (divergent interests, divided loyal ties, individual survival practices, diverse culture, Stockholm syndrome, etc.) the Filipinos did not have a sense of pre-colonizers' sense of nationhood, a heritage of "collective consciousness" nor a "collective unconscious," as something to fall back on and as a unifying force to pick themselves up from ashes of colonialism, the destruction and displacement caused by the revolution of 1896, the Filipino American war, WWII; disorientation and disorder of the post WWI period; widespread human rights violations of Marcos dictatorship and his destruction of the democratic institutions; and, the return and vengeance of the oligarchs, dynasties and elites.

But beyond the physical damage to the nation, the damage to the peoples' psyche was probably even worse. Successive defeats exacted their toll on the morale of the people, on their self-esteem, their self-confidence in forging their future. We became dependent, too complacent, too inept in negotiating with other countries; it was as if we lost our nerve and verve; we fell easily in identifying and conflating our national interest with other nations; we were lulled to stupor to the siren song of "special relations." We failed to envisage a **national vision.**

At the individual level, we see this lack of sense of nationhood. It's every man for himself or herself. To cite just one example, nobody beats us in personal hygiene and the general cleanliness of our homes. But step out of our home and see the filth in the street, sidewalk, waterways. People simply throw things into the public spaces or a neighbor's backyard. Nobody gives a damn. Our canals serve as garbage dump, clogging them up, so when the rain comes, flooding invariably ensues, causing damage to properties, disrupting business, and worse, endangering peoples' lives. These are physical damages; the damages to the Filipino psyche are equally devastating, if not far worse: despair, fatalism, sense of hopelessness, lack of confidence, lack of discipline, loss of initiative, dependency, lack of healthy regard for the public good and rule of law. This sense of disorder is reflected in our political life.

This idea and insight was brought home to me when I had been to Hawaii on a few occasions. I was struck that before the foreigners arrived, Kamehameha I through the force of his personality and leadership and peerless prowess as a soldier he consolidated all of Hawaiian fiefdoms before the British came and they were able to repulse them. When the Americans came, they were a solid kingdom, but because of the confluence of commercial interest and military strategic significance backed up by superior American forces, America easily occupied Hawaii and annexed it as the 50th state of the nation. Even as an annexed state, one still feels a strong undercurrent of native Hawaiian culture. If the American would leave Hawaii, the Hawaiian culture and identity would surely assert itself.

Much of the success of other countries such as Japan, Korea, China and India to recover from their colonial past was the buried native culture, past "collective unconscious" and past "collective consciousness" as a nation from which they were able to remember and able to draw upon to rise from the ashes of colonialism, to unite them, giving them again a sense of common bond, common purpose and dream and to move on as a people; they didn't have to struggle about identity as it had always been there, if buried, but easily came to the surface once they unshackled themselves from the chain of colonialism. They regained their pride, their self-esteem, their self-worth.

The British was a colonial power that colonized much of Africa and the Middle East. They partitioned the land not along ethno-linguistic lines, but purposely drew the line such that each country or "nation-state" was constituted by different ethnic groups or tribes to ensure that they would not come together as a nation for a long, long time so that their conquerors would go on to benefit the spoils of colonization. This was a recipe for conflict between and among the tribes, a situation that continues to this day in that part of the world.

The Philippines was not partitioned that way, but it may be said that we were partitioned in a way as destructive, if not more so, in the partitioning of our emerging national psyche, which to this day has not been made whole into a national psyche or national consciousness strong enough to propel our nation forward to prosperity.

Globalization & "Flatter World"

The world is shrinking. With globalization, "flatter world" and advances in communications and travel technology you have freer movement of goods, people and capital. The four-five decades have seen our people getting out of the country to greener pastures abroad and to seek personal fulfillment and personal fortune. The economy has not generated enough jobs for them to make a decent living. It's now estimated that there are about 11 million Filipinos working abroad in every corner of the world, in Africa, Middle East, Europe, Australia, Japan, Taiwan, Korea, US, Canada, etc.

Though the Filipinos have left the country they haven't really forgotten their home country. Every year thousands of them come for a visit to their home country and their families. Even when they could not personally travel back, their homeland is not far from their mind. In fact, in many places now around the world, with just a flick of remote, they can see life in the Philippines in real time; they could watch Philippine movies, music, talk shows, etc. With just click or tap on their smartphone, laptop, tablet or notebook, they could access online news about the Philippines; with social media such Facebook, YouTube, twitter, they could be in touch with their relatives back home; they could be in communication in real time with audio and video modes. Home is the Philippines even when literally it's not home anymore. For "home is where the heart is."

In their sojourn abroad, they have adopted to the life in the countries they immigrated to. Still, no matter how long they have been away, for most their Filipino-ness has not deserted them. In fact, in their interaction with a variety of peoples in faraway lands, they could not help but see themselves different from them and more sharply so. This could only accentuate their own sense of uniqueness as Filipinos.

Paradoxically, the advances in travel and communications technology by which they left the country are the very same technology that could bring them back or closer to home. I believe that this is also true for Filipinos at home. Ethno-linguistic factors and geographic dispersion were, among other things, factors in Filipinos not congealing together. These same technologies also bring closer together. The process could only accelerate as the cost of these technologies get cheaper.

I'm confident that elusive Filipino identity with its implications for a more cohesive nation and possibilities for united action and purpose will not be far from attainment.

So, to Nick Joaquin's remarks, "The Filipino identity is in the process of becoming," can be added, "It will become sooner than you think." Then the Filipino can dream the Filipino dream and realize it.

Life, like art, can be made whole and beautiful from broken pieces or ordinary items of existence. A Filipino nation can be forged that way. We have been dealt with a good share of lemons in our long history out of which we can make a lemonade.

(Note: The only other doctor I remember who'd give such a report was my senior resident in neurology at the UPCM-PGH when I did my rotation in that division during internship. His consultation notes would start with the history, then physical exam, review of tests and procedures results, followed by set of differential diagnoses and recommendations as to farther tests/procedures and treatment. He did not only make a list of differential diagnoses, from the most probable to least probable but a discussion of each differential diagnosis with citations from textbooks and journal articles, and treatment recommendations which would include advice on precautions and adverse reactions. Reading his notes was always a learning experience, much like you obtain from a book and medical journals, and would inspire to know more, thus, to do further research in the medical literature own your own. Beyond that was the discussion that it stimulated between and among the would-be doctors, the main beneficiary would the patients.)

2
UP. CBA, & Cesar Virata

Dateline: June 18, 2013

The University of the Philippines is unique and privileged institution of higher learning in the Philippines. It has been declared the "national university" of the Philippines; as such it has enjoyed academic freedom as no other college or university in the country. It has finally won its own charter, no longer subject to much of the bureaucratic red-tape of most colleges or universities under CHED or the Department of Education. Under its charter it's no longer subject to the standardized salary scale law, which permits it to provide slightly higher salaries for its faculties, slowing the bleeding of its talented professors to other schools. It is, of course, almost exclusively funded by the state and nominal tuition fee from students so much so that, to the common *tao* the acronym UP has meant University of the People.

In a word, the university has a great deal of latitude in academic and administrative matters, enabling it to concentrate on its core mission to educate the youth, transmit and push the frontiers of knowledge with the ultimate objective of helping in the development and growth of the nation for the greatest good of the greatest number of our people.

Its mission, although implicitly, not explicitly, articulated, and not openly taught, but subliminally conveyed through its general education program that includes the arts and humanities courses, is nevertheless, as a matter of first principles, guided by moral and ethical values and ideals.

UP has exceptionally succeeded in its academic mission, having produced most of the leaders of the country in any field, from the executive, legislative, judiciary branches of government, and in the private sector and any spheres of the nation's life. Sadly, among these leaders, UP has produced plenty of leaders who have led with less than sterling integrity and character. Indeed, two of its best and brightest alumni had been driven out from office, the first by People Power, and the second was nearly impeached but for her stranglehold on the concentrated state power and unlimited access to government coffers, but, thankfully, now under indictment for plunder and grave abuses of presidential powers. There are countless number of these corrupt and corrupted leaders whose hands are in control of governmental levers of power and in the private sector, dominated by oligarchs, who had been the product of UP.

When they were students at UP they were the epitome of youthful idealism, always at the forefront of defending national sovereignty and national interests. Rizal, one imagines, would be immensely proud of the them. Yet, yet, many, if not majority of them, once they stepped out of the portals to the university, immediately get absorbed in and be part of the dysfunctional system. I was as if they had developed sudden amnesia about their personal and national ideals.

One of the brightest lights that was a product of UP education in whom the hopes and dreams of an entire nation was reposed on was Ferdinand Marcos. Initially the people indeed thought he was the "messiah" who would deliver them to the "promise land." His mantra was "we can be great again." And the people bought into it ecstatically.

He recruited the best and the brightest of the Filipinos to carry out his program of government. And among this select few of "the best and the brightest" was the outsized and dazzling star of the firmament: Cesar Emilio Aguinaldo Virata, engineer par excellence, but found his ultimate calling in the financial world before he became the dean of the College of Business Administration. He transformed that college into one of the respected and prestigious components of the university.

It soon became evident, though, that Marcos lost his way or had other designs for the nation. In one fell swoop he "transformed" the nation. To make the story short, he destroyed practically all democratic institutions of the government. He made himself a dictator; he revised the Constitution to give him more powers; he and his cronies looted and plundered the coffers of the government; Imelda was his partner-in-crime in this; he virtually instituted a police state. He and his surrogates cut short countless lives, mostly the youth, whose flowering was about to emerge and to fully bloom; impoverished the Filipino people, on top of which he left them and the nation a staggering debt of around $ 60-80 billion; his conjugal partner regularly raided the Central Bank when she went on shopping spree around the world, especially in New York City; when he and his family finally were ousted by People Power and exiled to Hawaii he had stashed billions of dollars and gold abroad. In fact, just recently the Marcos family offshore wealth was estimated at $ 5-10 billion with staggering amount of gold, 6.3 metric tons. It's not clear if this gold loot is included in that $ 5-10 billion or in addition to it.

Where was Virata all along during this period? He was a loyal, servile technocrat. He assumed many positions, but especially stood out as secretary of fiance and at some point Prime Minister and chief negotiator for loans from various international multilateral financial institutions. Such high government positions gave him unprecedented and special access to all government financial, banking institutions and big business transactions, negotiations. And he must also had access also to other irregularities in governance, including security and military matters. Did he raise any objection to all the shenanigans, abuses of power, corrupt practices in private or in public? Not that we know of. In some circles he was reported to have submitted his resignation on more than one occasion, but rejected by the president. We don't know how true these were. There are resignations and *resignations*. If one is truly determined to resign, one must assume that he can actually do so with legitimate excuses like health, exhaustion and there is always the family to fall back on.

Thus one is tempted to think and to conclude that such gestures of resignation were feigned. It is not far-fetched to imagine that in resigning but not really resigning *hubris* was at work, believing that he alone can do the job or save the Philippines, a sense of indispensability. What a lame excuse and rationalization. At UP, not to mention at other schools, there were so many smart if not brilliant people whose probity was beyond question, who could easily have stepped into his job(s). He could not possibly be delusional that he was the only Filipino who can deliver. Or, was he?

Much was/is made of the his supposed virtue of honesty, that he never amassed much wealth and he lived/lives modestly. Okay, let us grant all this. Not all is indeed motivated by money or wealth. Not all is motivated by pomp, glory and circumstance. Not all is motivated by power, although that is a rare individual indeed. But let's look under the hood, so to speak, of this virtuous man.

It is not unreasonable to imagine that underneath all this appearance or reality of virtues was/is a deeper motive, consciously or subconsciously, namely, a sense of being extremely jealous of protecting his reputation from being tarnished. It is equally plausible that his supposed virtues were tainted or masked by remarkable selfishness, especially when these are set against the gross abuses of power and corruption that surrounded him, that were destroying the people and nation. "People and the nation be damned as long as I keep my good name, along as I am not an active participant." Many times, there is a thin line that separates virtues from "un-virtues" or foibles and vices.

If not that, it suggests, as alternative explanation, that Virata was in the mold of super-efficient robotic technocrat, cold, detached individual, unfeeling to the sorry and sordid state of the people and nation, programmed by his Boss, and followed the program to the T, not unlike in the manner of the German generals who claimed to be merely following orders. He fits aptly the proverbial three monkeys who "see no evil, hear no evil, and speak no evil." Or, to repeat an oft-quoted dictum, "The only thing necessary for the triumph of evil is good men to do nothing."

One can also say that the reason he did not really stepped down in the manner of the truly distinguished men of impeccable integrity and character and extraordinary talents like Vicente Paterno and Rafael Salas was he lacked moral courage and backbone.

There is no doubt in the minds of countless people that in choosing to stay with Marcos, he helped propped him up because of his name in the international financial institutions, from which the regime massively borrowed money to keep the nation afloat, but from which it was also drowning in debt. Had he abandoned Marcos, the latter's fall could have happened much sooner. The same can be said of Carlos P. Romulo, but that is another story (Romulo reportedly had bedside conversion, but severe damage to the nation had been done by then).

In the minds of many--on behalf of tens of hundreds if not thousands of the voiceless who gave the "last full measure of devotion" to country and alma mater and of those who suffered degraded lives, poverty, hunger even starvation, poor or no education, hardly a roof over their heads, clothes over their frail bodies --"tinimbang siya, ngunit kapos na kapos siya." He served his master with outmost loyalthy and effciency, but hardly anything for his people. He did/does not deserve the honor. The only decent and honorable for him to do is to decline the tribute bestowed on him by the College of Business Administration and the Univesity of the Philippines.

In the final analysis, the question of Virata is one of morality and ethics. In my view, shared by many people-- graduates and non-graduates of UP-- what was committed in naming the College of Business Administration [the school that embodies its academic program and integrity, the faculty, the ethos of the college (and of the the university), and not just the bricks and stones, as asserted by some] was a gross transgression of moral and ethical standards, for it implicitly or explicitly endorsed, or at least ignored, the norm of behavior of Virata when he had served from beginning to the end of Marcos regime.

UP cannot hide under the guise of academic freedom, in the name of its independence as embodied in its new Charter. After all it is still supported financially by the people/the nation, to whom it is unquestionably accountable, and for whom it made a solemn contract to advance their interest above any consideration, and from whom its very existence derives from their hopes and aspirations

It's time, long overdue, for UP not only to worship under the shrine of the mind, but in the shrine of moral and ethical values and principles and dictates of the heart.

3
The Clash of Civilizations: My Take

Dateline: 2013

Both, seemingly paradoxical, but that's what the world is.

I read the "The Clash of Civilizations" by Samuel Huntington many years ago, which clash keeps our dear friend Prof. Cesar sleepless in California. As I recall, if such Clash happens, it will not happen between the Centers of power, but at the periphery, between and among the client or surrogate states; but before that stage is reached the super powers would have taken more than adequate measures to prevent such escalation to their level. They are not suicidal; each knows the the capability of the other; they know they could blow up the world many times over even with existing weapons system, themselves included. Remember MAD; its not passe. Any major meeting/conference such as the one between US & China recently, is both summitry and gimmickry. Both super powers are playing to the world and to their respective constituency. This is more to it than meets the eye. The two are so closely interwoven and intertwined on many issues that they cannot live together, yet they could not live apart. That's their *modus vivendi.* They thus engaged in doublespeak, not so much their words are necessarily internally contradictory as they are "perverse" complementarity, or one can go further, "unitary message" in the larger scheme of of things. In the lower scale of things there is the appearance of contradiction, if not clash of positions. Following this logic, it is not unexpected that North Korea is a done deal even before the summit. In the same vein, the same is true of the brouhaha in the South China sea and proximate body of water, e.g., the one between Japan and China, etc. Most of their press releases are merely posturing to appease their respective audience at home and to project an image to the world for so-called credibility, which should not be dismissed. But on essential and fundamental matters, I suspect, there is already some sort of agreeable agreement even before. It's like two good lawyers. Each doesn't a question to which they don't already know the answer (right. Atty. and Sen. Saguisag?)

In a sense, recall the days of old, for a rough analogy, the Age of Exploration and Colonization. I'm in particular referring to the two super powers then, Spain and Portugal, that struck a deal (or dictated or mediated by the pope then), divvying the known world into tow spheres: one for you, one for me. And for a long time it worked, until other nations wanted to have part of the pie, so to speak (e.g., Britain, Germany, Belgium, etc.). The world is full of peoples predisposed to covetousness. Envy, as much as altruistic impulse, resides in the human heart as well as in the human head (mind, reason; what appeal to reason?!!! That has been debunked so many times as much by experiential existence as cognitive psychology and neuroscience. That's why the Age of Enlightenment or Reason was followed by the Romantic backlash...in the art, philosophy, music, etc. Such is the state of the Homo Sapience. Left to his own devices, he's likely to self-destruct. Thus the need for higher power or state: Grace or State of Grace. "But for Thy grace, there go I," the adage goes. It's true. Simply look around and plenty to support this thesis. Thus, recognizing my puniness and phoniness at times, I believe in appealing to a Higher Power and Authority, God.Nothing, nothing can can convince me otherwise. If there were no God, I'd invent Him. But no need for such presumptiveness. For I already believe in Him, as sure as the sun will rise tomorrow, as Annie would sing, act and dance it. Ah, where am I? Oh yes, on "Clash of Civilizations."

Getting on track, the cyberhacking...don't you believe it. Each has been spying on each other for as long as anyone cares, and both masters of the world know it. (Masters of Wall Street & Big Business are entirely different species. They can't take it with them, anyway. And as my favorite economist would say, "In the long run, we'll all be dead." If there were not enough to scare them, the Good Book says it more emphatically and straightforwardly, "From dust thou cometh, to dust doth return." Nick Joaquin, arguably the greatest of our all-around writer in English put it so graphically; I don't remember the title of the poem and forgot all the the lines. but to paraphrase it: Even Kings for all their power, pomp and glory, will someday, not too far in the horizon, will turn to no more that fertilizers for cabbage, among other possibilities.

And so, my dear friend Prof. Cesar, don't worry too much about "Clash of Civilizations." May you sleep tight tonight. There is a Higher Power---above atheists, agnostics, believers---who cares for you and me. "That's all you need to know, that's all you need to now."

4
On Manufacturing in USA

Dateline: Sept. 2013 - comments posted online

Chay, Congratulations for a very well written piece. Your enthusiasm is almost contagious; I say almost, because your optimism for return of manufacturing is less than persuasive and compelling. You say manufacturing is returning to America because it will return. Hmm. That seems to me a tautological argument and therefore circular or enclosed in a loop. You would have been more effective in you assertion if you've provided us with the reasons that under-gird it.

Short of empirical facts or evidence, I'd say that your thesis is sort of intuitive in character, which nonetheless should not be dismissed, for in fact some intuitions are later found to have factual basis.

Indeed, your intuition is not without factual foundation. I recently read an article (I don't remember where I read it; maybe the NYT) that the US export is quite factually robust; much of this export is manufacturing-based. The forecast is that this will accelerate in the coming years based on the trend so far. As I recall, there are three factors why manufacturing is seeing a rebirth in America: Newly discovered enormous gas reserve upgrading/ upgraded power grid, both which should lower energy cost; and, shipping cost getting steeper. Also, there is, I think, another factor at play which was not mentioned in the article but read it from a recent book, "Fate of the States: The New Geography of American Prosperity." The author argues that the meltdown of the economy in 2008 and its aftershocks affected mainly the coastal states, but the heartland of America (except the traditional manufacturing states such as Michigan, Ohio, etc) hardly suffered in terms of deficits, have more money for infrastructure and investment on education; in these states the wage scale is much lower than in the coastal states. Therefore, they stand ready to take advantage of the rebound of the economy more than the "moribund" states.

Also, the advances in technology (especially robotics) do not pose as much problem as initially thought; the net effect is that advanced technology, while conferring the highest benefit to the highly educated, skilled individuals, will create jobs that's between the high end and the low end, much like manufacturing jobs used to provide, a boon to the middle class. The article on this came out of NYT last week.

So, your intuition is not without basis in facts. That should all cheer us up. Now, if only the GOPs in the fringes are not constantly putting obstacle courses, happy days should be here again!

Now as to your other countries doing their own thing about manufacturing, I agree with you.

It would be a world with multiple poles of economic prosperity, based on manufacturing, which in turn is anchored by high science and technology along with low-wage workers. In a sense, the future scenario is de-globalization running in parallel with globalization. In other words, it's no longer one way street. It's much like "a thousand flowers in bloom." Wouldn't that be beautiful!

5
Power & Empowerment

Dateline: 2014

[9] What has been will be again,
what has been done will be done again;
there is nothing new under the sun.

[10] Is there anything of which one can say,
"Look! This is something new"?.
It was here already, long ago;
it was here before our time.
Ecclesiastes

For sure nothing is new here, but reshuffling the deck offers
new perspective and insight

Myriad Problems

Filipinos know the reality that the Philippines has
fallen far behind economically with its Asian neighbors, now
with Vietnam overcoming us, Cambodia right on our heels,
Bangladesh pulling about even, and Myanmar (Burma)
showing on our rear-view mirror. To mention Japan, Korea,
Taiwan, Singapore, Thailand, Malaysia and Indonesia is
superfluous.

Results

It's being an economic laggard is manifested in
myriad ways: widespread poverty and malnutrition;
inadequate or broken infrastructure (roads, bridges, ports,
airports, etc.); power short, erratic and expensive (one of the
highest in Asia); inaccessible health care system for majority
of its citizens with dismal health indices; substandard basic
education; high level of unemployment and under-
employment; social ills such as drug addiction; drug and
human trafficking; rampant smuggling; pervasive corruption

at all levels of govt. and in the private sector, ad infinitum ad nauseam.

Causes

The above list comes readily to mind as the consequences or results of our lack-luster economic performance, but can easily be conceived of as the causes or contributing causes of it in a manner of negative feedback loop. We are thus thrown off guard to think clearly of our societal problems, confusing causes and results, unable come up with credible and effective solutions.

Ghosts of the Past

In this state of mental unclarity we sometimes grasp at straws or ghosts of the past. We take refuge in the past, nostalgic at the good old days, rhapsodizing about past glory as when we were number two, second only to Japan in economic development, as when our national university, UP, ranked one of the finest institutions in the region, etc.

In this mindset, but in darker mood, we fall into re-litigating old controversies or re-fighting old battles, as for example debating endlessly and uselessly the issue of Rizal's retraction; second guessing ourselves if indeed Rizal should have been our national hero, not sure if Rizal advocated absolute independence from Spain or did he merely demand major reforms from Spain and representation in the Spanish Cortes, but still to be under the governance of Spain; arguing whether Bonifacio should have been the national hero, who after all mounted the armed revolution against Spain for decisive break and total independence against all odds, etc. These are just few of the questions that torture our souls, exhausting our energies for constructive actions for the gargantuan problems our nation faces today.

Lofty Ideals

Unable to wrap ourselves around realistic and pragmatic solutions, there is the appeal to lofty and higher ideals as if indulging ourselves in them will solve our all too real and immediate problems. We wax poetic with truth, justice, liberty, etc. in the abstract, seldom in concrete terms that make them susceptible to practical and down-to-earth solutions.

Anybody but...

Then there is that all too familiar trait of us to blame anybody but ourselves, of not taking personal responsibility for our own actions, this confounded by our own inability to think beyond self, oblivious to our obligations to promoting the greater good of the whole, of the body politic of which we are a apart.

Cast in stone, rearranging the deck

We are stuck in a mental prison that looks at our problems in the old fashion way, repeating old stale approaches that offer the same failed results. The mold needs to be broken. We need a fresh conceptual framework with which to view our national problems, that offer the possibility of bringing creative and innovative ways to bear on them..

Power & Empowerment

It is suggested that we look at our problems in the concept and reality of power. Now that might cause some people to pause thinking that it's something radical involving the use of force. It's far from it. It is certainly bold but it makes for clarity and immediacy of thinking; it concentrates the mind and compels purposeful action.

Reflecting on power, one can easily conjure up the power of the atom, its power to do good or to do evil. Because we're normally rational men and women, we unleash its power in controlled manner and harness its power for constructive purposes. In the same manner, in the societal area, it's envisioned only that the political, economic and social power be unleashed for constructive purposes and in controlled way.

At bottom the central problem of our nation is power, especially political and economic power. That power is skewed and concentrated. It is often abused, leveraged for those who have the fingers on the lever of power for their own selfish interests -- the common people be damned! Simply put: the central problem is allocation of power...concentrated, manipulated and benefiting only the few in society.

The logical solution, therefore, is the proper allocation of power, to distribute it as broadly as possible, to make it more inclusive, to make sure it is not captured by any narrow, special groups that perpetrate the "iron law of oligarchy."

Power broadened

In the birth and organization of a society or a nation, the first step is a political act, i.e., to arrive at consensus on who is to lead and to exercise power and authority, and the extent and limitation of the powers he/she exercises. This is not just a question of conferring power on somebody or groups of individuals but to legitimize it and on whom it may be exercised and under what circumstances and parameters.

Political Power: fettered & organized

But even as power and authority are conferred and delegated to the leaders and shared with as broad a distribution as possible to attain pluralism, there should be an accompanying centralizing and organizing principle such that such power is not dissipated, wasted, wild and out of control. It should be within the scope of the law.

Reference was made to the power of the atom. We only make use of its constructive power when that power is unleashed in a controlled manner. In similar fashion, political power should be decentralized, but should still be within the domain of an organizing and centralizing principle. In terms of political power that would mean the power should be within the parameters of the rule of law. Otherwise, the power could easily be hijacked by certain sectors of the body politic, amassing more power unto themselves, used for their own selfish interests. Also, it might give undue autonomy to disparate groups that the distributed power is incapable to be gathered together, when the occasion calls for it, for larger collective action for the good of the whole or the entire nation. You don't want a balkanization of the nation, each group pulling whichever way and working at cross-purposes with other groups.

Alternative: Federal System

The structure of our government is the presidential form with its three main branches (executive, legislative and judiciary) for more than fifty years; the three branches are designed for differentiated and differential functions, and to provide checks and balances in the exercise of political power. It is more than obvious that it has failed us miserably; it has failed to prevent the concentration and abuse of power.

It's time to consider seriously the federal form of government. First and foremost, it decentralizes power to different regions, which would empower each federal unit to chart its own programs of government, no longer too dependent on the central government in Manila. It provides more autonomy for those regions, freeing them to devise more innovative and creative ways to deal with challenges of their region. Because the seat of power in such a schema is closer to the people, the latter could more readily access it not only to voice their grievances, but enable them to monitor the actions of their leaders and to contribute more directly to creative and innovative solutions to the problems of governance, to provide solutions from ground up that are likely to be more relevant to their daily lives, rather laboring under the dictates from above which in many occasions prove impractical and expensive to implement.

Under a federal form of govt. each region, although far more autonomous, is still under the reach of the federal government as dictated by the rule of law or set of laws embodied in the rules and regulations that define the relations between the states or regions and the federal (central) govt.

In connection with the decentralization of power, it's good to think in terms of institutionalizing it, i.e., to make it across the board and lend it support with any and every legal means to make it endure. With this we form "virtuous circles" that should move forward toward us a more prosperous and just nation.

Whether there should also be a shift to a parliamentary govt...that I leave to our political scientists; I'm not sufficiently knowledgeable to give an informed opinion.

Grand Jury & Trial Jury

Adoption of the Grand Jury and the Trial Jury System is a major advance in leveling the playing field in the distribution of and exercise of power. The current system we have is often subverted or corrupted by those in power. Those who wield political and economic power not infrequently get their way either by buying it or through intimidation. With the Grand Jury and Trial Jury, people are judged by their own peers, who normally share their life experiences and concerns, who use the same language, at the same educational and cultural level. The members of the jury could identify more easily with their plight and concerns, more attuned and sensitive to their grievances. Because decisions are shared more widely and collectively they are less susceptible to dictates from above or from the judgment of one man or limited number of men, who by their education and cultural values are usually detached from those of the common people. In this format, the deck is much less stacked against the common man and he/she is better able to obtain true justice.

Freedom of Information (FOI)

On several occasions, activities, transactions and policy decisions in government, in cahoots with the

political and power elites in the country, are done in the dark. This is most conducive to corruptions that permeate our society. It provides access to asymmetric information that gives those in power to have undue advantage over the common people. This leads to practices that dissipate public coffers or looting of governmental resources and other abuses, e.g., administration of justices. It slows down considerably the completion of needed projects that benefit the people. A good example is the construction of the NAIA3 which started in Pres. Ramos term and continues to present; up to now it's less than 50 % operational. Billions and billions of public money have been lost, not to mention the loss of economic benefits that would have accrued to the nation and our people had it been in full operation from days 1 of its supposed completion and operation.

It's more than evident, therefore, that light be shone where darkness exists to substantially minimize, if not completely eradicate, the corrupt practices and activities of people in government. A Freedom of Information, institutionalized in the form a law, can go a long way in bringing transparency and light to public officials nefarious activities.

Education

Oftentimes power is not unilaterally granted, but must be demanded. A big prerequisite to this demand for and obtaining it is to know one's rights and prerogatives. This requires education. It is important that the citizens should be provided with good, useful basic education, to know their civic duties and rights and obligations of citizenship. That education should also include technical/ vocational or higher education that allows the individual to obtain knowledge and skills that make for a decent living either as an employee or self-employed; people with gainful employment are less intimidated and more assertive of their rights.

Old Wine, Late Bloom

Our educational system and policies should not only provide quality education but education that is relevant, that is, aligned with what is available in the marketplace to maximize the likelihood that the individual gets gainful employment or has the skills for self-employment.

Our educational leaders and political and economic leaders many times are working at cross-purposes; students in some courses have been allowed to multiply like rabbit even when the market for such their professions has been severely contracted. The nursing profession is a good example, where tens of thousands of nurses found themselves jobless. The nursing course had gotten out of control; the tuition had gotten out of line, costing like PhP 60,000.00 per semester, compared to other courses like engineering, computer science, accounting where the tuition is around Php 20,000.00 per semester.

We hear stories of hospitals exploiting them; to get clinical experience in a hospital, the nursing graduate has to pay the hospital, sometimes at exorbitant fee; it used to be the other way around, the hospital paying stipend to the nursing graduate.

Our educational system should emphasize science and technology. In all developed economies there is a robust science and technology-based education; we should emulate this, because it underpins our drive for economic development. This feature allows us to withstand "creative destruction" and to innovate without which society stagnates and becomes easy prey to those ensconced in power and who arrogate unto themselves more political and economic power. A nation of educated people (in technical, vocational or higher education) are not easily swayed or bought by unscrupulous political and economic elites. They also make for the nation in "competitive advantage," in the words of Michael Porter and Thomas Friedman, in a globalized economy and "flatter world."

Economic Power

Heretofore we've been discussing mainly political power. But of course political power is linked inextricably with economic power, which could form negative or positive feedback loop, depending how it's used: "extractive" political and economic institutions," or "inclusive" political and economic institutions. The former enslave and impoverish, the latter liberate and lead to social justice, empowerment and better economic life.

It's often difficult to make heads and tails of political power and economic power, the two like being conjoined twins. Nevertheless, it's probably convenient for practical and theoretical purposes to think first of political power.

For in the formation of society or a nation, what comes first is the political question. In order to wield power one needs to settle first from which it springs and derives it authority. In submitting that question, one necessarily seeks its social nature. In other words, in order for it to be legitimate it seeks validation from the people it hopes to lead and rule.

Only when that is settled that the exercise of economic power can be legitimate. In other words, economic power flows from the legitimate political power. For it's in the nature of economic power that it's oftentimes private; that cannot be the sole basis of substantial economic power especially as it serves mainly private gain. It must not be in conflict with the larger purpose of society, albeit it should be given as much latitude as possible, but only to the extent that it doesn't jeopardize the larger interest of the whole, especially because, given its power it can easily hijack and capture political power. It should be given much latitude as reasonably possible because in the ultimate analysis, the seat of creativity and innovation is in the individual; much of economic activity, at least initially, stems from individual effort and talent.

Language

Finally, in order for society or nation to organize organically, it should endeavor to cultivate one national language even as it fosters other major languages in the land. These languages reflect the soul of the people, allow them to discourse with one another in a manner only they can truly understand and identify with each other. It's disconcerting to observe how often our leaders would give speeches in highfalutin language before an audience who barely have a basic education and do not have a handle on the language the speaker is using. There's not merely something is lost in the translation, but they, the political leaders and the common people, are really interacting past each other's head. Beyond that there is the perception the leader can be or is condescending.

This project has to be done long-term as not to be disruptive of the current curriculum, as the latter is presently undergoing much makeover already. It can be a project for next fifty years. For now, the school system can offer the national language as a course study in elementary, secondary and college levels; the same could be done for other major languages. In the meantime, we can continue with English as the medium of instruction for pragmatic reasons from grade 4 up with the mother tongue of the child used as the medium instruction from K to grade 3 (see MTBMLE).

Media, Social Network, & NGOs

In this enterprise the media have to be fully engaged. They wield enormous power and if properly used they can do tremendous good for the people and transform our society for a more just, open and equitable society. They can be the eyes and ears of the people, they can spot and expose abuses of power, anomalies and waste in government, see to it that justice is served. They can make use of the traditional means of print or broadcast media, or make use of the new social media, like Facebook, YouTube, Twitter.

The public now can also avail themselves of the new media and social network to safeguard the interests of the public and to expose anomalous practices, to mobilize for collective action, much like the Arab spring in Egypt, Tunisia and Libya and Syria. The many NGOs, better organized, must continue with their commitment to the social good utilizing the reach and power of the new communications technology.

The whole idea is to restructure the political and economic power to bring about economic development in an inclusive manner, as broad as possible, to serve the greatest good of the greatest number of people.

6
Philippine Economic Development: Consciousness, Spirit and Vision

Dateline: 1986

The Twenty-first Century is almost upon us. It has been called the "Pacific Rim Century." This is not an empty catch phrase. Witness the latest economic boom, namely, that of China which is growing at a fast clip of thirteen percent per annum. The economic miracles of Korea, Taiwan, Hong Kong, Singapore and Thailand are also well known. And, of course, Japan is the prototype of the economic miracle of the East Asia region.

The Philippines is a unit – indeed lies at the very center – of that region. Sadly, we remain invisible in that prosperity map of East Asia.

There was a time, in the 50s and early 60s, however, when we were at the leading edge of economic activity in that part of the world, second only to Japan. This period saw the beginning of industrialization and entrepreneurship in the Philippines.

But evidently we have faltered and have fallen far behind our Asian neighbors. This need not be our permanent lot.

By the accident of geography, we are right there at the center of the Pacific Rim -- where the economic dynamism is. We are at the crossroads of the commercial air and sea lanes to and from the Pacific and the world. We can be the hub of commerce and trade in the Pacific. Our proximity to the vibrant and booming economies of the Pacific and Asia should, logically, rub off on the Philippines, infusing some vitality to our economic life. In real estate parlance--as it could be in economic development-- location, location, location is a key asset. And we are right at it.

But geography, in and by itself, one does not sufficiently guarantee our becoming a major participant in the economic boom of the region. Advances in telecommunications, including the touted information highway, and travel can easily bypass us. We cannot be like Juan Tamad waiting for the guava fruit to fall into his lap.

We have to climb the tree, indeed, the mountain where the tree is. We cannot be passive. We have to seek out and seize opportunities. We have, with the help of God, to forge our own future. Otherwise, the Twenty First Century will just pass us by, as did the Twentieth Century.

But why and how did we falter? What went wrong? What accounts for our economic stagnation, and in fact, retrogression? What is it in us, in our character that prevented us from moving forward and keeping pace with our Asian neighbors? What external forces stalled our economic development?

Let us now consider some of them:

PART I: CONVENTIONAL WISDOM

Almost invariably when you pose the above questions to Filipinos, the first thing that comes to their mind is corruption. It seems the Filipinos drink, eat and breathe corruption. Listening to our compatriots, you get the impression that we must be the most corrupt people in the world. Corruption is indeed pervasive in our society, and it is a sad commentary on our people, especially because we take pride in proclaiming ourselves to be the only Christian nation in Asia. Obviously, there is a disconnect between our Christian faith and how we live our faith. Nevertheless, I do not believe that we have a monopoly of it. I do not believe that we are any worse or any better than other people on this matter.

While nobody should condone corruption and everybody must fight it vigorously, let us not fail to note that graft and corruption have not stopped the economic-miracle nations from moving ahead phenomenally.

Corruption cannot adequately explain our economic failure. Let us not make corruption a convenient pretext for our failure.

The issue of corruption is just one of the many challenges we face. Even as we fight it strenuously, let us make sure we have more that enough energy left for more creative and productive endeavors. We cannot, should not, tackle corruption to the exclusion of everything else. Neither should we let it render us so dispirited to the point of hopelessness, helplessness or inaction.

National discipline is another ready response. We're not a disciplined people, many will say. In contrast, the Japanese and the Germans are held as prime examples of discipline. Discipline, admittedly, is not one of our strong points. On the other hand, we're free-spirited people who have the capacity to endure and roll with the punches, and to enjoy life even in times of adversity. This congeniality of spirit makes us relate to other people with ease.

Discipline, especially one of rigidity, cannot be everything. It can lead to dogmatism, authoritarianism, or even worse, totalitarianism that could threaten the fabric of free society and the world. This is not to say that we, Filipinos, could not benefit from a little discipline in our national life. For discipline has a lot to do in the ordering not only of our individual lives but our national life, including our national economic life.

Some would find fault with our work ethic; these critics would make the quick comparison again with the Japanese, Germans and Koreans. We don't work hard enough like these people do, they say. I thought this argument was adequately refuted by Rizal in his essay, "The Indolence of the Filipinos." I don't believe this charge one bit. Look at our farmers, peasants, factory workers: how they toil from dawn to dusk. Look at the Filipinos here in America: how they work so hard, a lot of them keeping two or three jobs, especially our nurses, who are heroically keeping the Philippine economy afloat with their dollar remittances. There could be no other people working so hard to provide for themselves, their families and their country.

An issue somewhat related to this is our alleged distaste for manual labor. It is often charged that we look down upon manual labor. We like the white collar jobs. Everybody wants to go to the university or college just so he or she can land a clerical or office job. Nobody wants to go to technical or vocational school because jobs of this nature are not considered glamorous, "respectable" or "dignified." There is some truth to this charge. How much it contributes to our uneconomic condition I am not sure. Intuitively, it must have a considerable impact in the spirit of entrepreneurship, the driving force for economic development and growth.

For to be an entrepreneur or starting businessman, one must be willing to dirty one's hands and do what is takes to succeed, especially if one is low on capital as it is often the case when one is starting and cannot afford to pay hired hands. It would be interesting to probe further into this cultural attitude but it is not within the scope of this article.

Some would question our lifestyle. It is asserted that we Filipinos are very lavish in our lifestyle.

Indeed, we are downright extravagant, living far above our means. We will get into a heavy debt to make a big splash for fiestas. Don't get me wrong. I believe in fiestas, contrary to the position taken by a Philippine senator who ran for president and who wanted to ban it altogether. Fiesta is social glue as important as our laws and can be a vehicle for creative and productive celebration. But there have to be limits to what we'll spend for it. We don't squander the family fortune to celebrate it, or at the expense of the family business. Another example: At Filipino social functions where some of the ladies would change their gowns not twice but three or four times for the same evening affair. This is downright as poor taste as it is obscene indulged in by the *nouveau riche.*

What does all this mean? We have one of the lowest savings rate as a nation. That's why we are in a black hole of debt (28 billion dollars and climbing). We do not have sufficient internal capital to fuel our economy as there is no national savings to speak of. "We live for today, never mind tomorrow"--that seems to be our motto. (It would interesting to probe the sociology of this issue but again it's beyond the scope of this article).

HOPE, PROMISE AND BETRAYAL

When Marcos came upon the scene, he proclaimed, "The Filipinos can be great again." With this slogan, he captured the enthusiasm and imagination of most Filipinos. People believed in their hearts that as their president he would deliver them to the promise land of economic prosperity. Initially, it seemed he would deliver on his promise. For Marcos had everything. He was brilliant. He was endowed with uncommon foresight, charisma and ability to connect with the common people with ease, even as he could comfortably engaged the learned and intellectuals in high-minded discourses. He wielded absolute power. He was capable of the grand vision as no previous Filipino president possessed and had the administrative talent to bring it to fruition. And he had the support of America during his term of office (except toward the end), which was a considerable asset. It was impossible for him to fail. But fail he did. In the process he took down the nation with him.

Never had a people been more hopeful. Never had a people felt more betrayed.

Marcos and company inflicted incalculable damage to our national life, especially our economic life.

The destruction of Philippine institutions during the Marcos regime of 21 years was a major factor in grinding down our economy to a level below that which we had reached in the 50s and 60s, before Marcos became president. It was during the Martial Law (1972-1980) and post-Martial-Law--but still dictatorial (1981-1986) period of this regime--that vital economic and social institutions were placed in the hands of Marcos cronies for their benefit no matter what the cost the nation and the Filipino people.

Here are a few examples. The banking system in the Philippines became a farce. The coconut industry from which a significant percentage of the population derived their income, and from which a great deal of entrepreneurs normally get their starting capital, was delivered by decree into the hands of a few cronies (some of them ruthless enough to assassinate their enemies, including an attempt on the life of former Ambassador to the U.S., Ambassdor Emmanuel Palaez). These coconut cronies controlled not only the ability of the coconut farmers to plant, but also the price they could sell the fruits of their labor and investment, and finally, the disposition of the dollars they earned when the coconut was sold abroad. Small producers of shoes and preserved food products were swallowed up by their competitors who were Marcos cronies, the latter having an edge because of their links to the banks and licensing and other authorities. Industrialists who were not Marcos partisans were hounded down, if not jailed.

The assassination of Benigno Aquino, which started the Marcos's fall, also triggered the period of intensified capital flight by Marcos cronies. Whereas before they were only salting away abroad what their enterprises earned, now – in the years between 1983 and 1986-- they converted even their peso assets into dollars, marks and yens and smuggled billions of these to their second homes in America, Europe and Asia. No other country save perhaps Haiti was depleted of its financial resources by the cronies of the failing and rapidly falling reigning power in this way.

Yet to blame Marcos and company entirely or mostly for our economic misery is to give them too much credit and, in a sense, to make them scapegoats for our *own failings*. It is a cop-out.

ADVENTURISM AND HUMAN FOLLY

Notwithstanding the devastation wrought by Marcos and company, the immediate post Marcos period was full of promise; we were on the road to a fast recovery. But just when we were to take off, misfortune struck again.

Perhaps many of us have actually forgotten that only five years ago, the Philippines nearly lost its democracy once more in the hands of the faction of the military that wished to impose their doctrine – similar to that of many failed and sorry colonels in South America and Africa – upon the Filipino people.

There were eight coup attempts on the government then led by Mrs. Corazon Aquino. All of these served to pull down the Philippines several rungs down the economic ladder. But the most disastrous one was the 1989 coup attempt that nearly toppled Mrs. Aquino's government.. Remember?

Well, this had a very destructive effect on the Philippine economy. For the fact is that in 1989, only three years after Marcos was booted out by the People's Power uprising in 1986, the Philippine economy had recovered to the level of the economy in 1981. This level was much higher that the nadir the economic had declined to in the late 1983-84-85, after the Aquino assassination that brought the economy, and perhaps even social life, almost to a standstill.

That in the late 1988 and from January to November 1989, so soon after 1986, and despite the interruption of the coup attempts, our poor depleted country had reached the 1981 level was something the American, European and Japanese bankers saw as a sign that indeed the Philippines was an economic tiger in the making. Because of this miraculous and speedy recovery, foreign investors with hundreds of millions of dollars had actually come in early 1989. Many had signed up with Philippine partners to infuse large doses of capital for various industrial and agribusiness projects. Small and medium-scale Filipino entrepreneurs who were crushed during the Marcos years, supported by a rehabilitated banking system, had again become active.

But then in December 1989 tragedy struck. The rebellious military group launched their most massive coup attempt. Many lives were lost. They succeeded in taking over some government installations and a TV station.

For a few days it looked as if the Philippine government would fall. Thankfully, with the confluence of events, it didn't..

The negative economic impact of the December 1989 coup had not been too widely discussed. Part of the reason is that the Philippine government financial and economic agency personnel themselves, as well as private sector Filipinos in banking industry, had downplayed it for a reason. Talking about it would only add to the scare in the minds of possible foreign investors.

What happened was this: U.S., European and some Hong Kong companies that had already invested in the Philippines pulled out of the Philippines. These included computer and garment manufacturers, banks such as Bank of America (which had its central offices for Southeast Asia in Manila) and tourism development investors. Foreign banks that had already signed agreements to support Philippines industry and agri-business with loans to Filipino or their foreign joint-venture partners withdrew. The net result was that in January 1990 – four and a half years ago – the Philippines was economically again in square one!

NATURE'S FURY

As if man-made disasters were not enough, nature—seeming intent to teach us some lesson and punish us for our own foolishness—unleashed its own fury, virtually making a wasteland of tens of thousands of hectares of the most productive land in the Philippines.

Mt. Pinatubo's fireworks, which was the immediate cause of the closure of the American military bases in Clark and Subic, did much more economic and social damage than the loss of jobs in these bases. The eruptions and the flow of the lava actually made towns and villages disappear. The site of Pinatubo's devastation is Central Luzon, the rice granary of the Philippines, which is also next to Metropolitan Manila area itself, the most densely populated and best-developed region industrially and economically. Major parts of Central Luzon was destroyed by Pinatubo and its aftermath; the entire Central Luzon was plunged into status of economically depressed zone, with tens of thousands, if not millions, rendered homeless, and thus, creating massive refugee problem.

THE LEGACY OF HISTORY

It is easy enough to identify the man-made and natural disasters that wrecked havoc to our economy, but there were more insidious and more elusive forces at work that can be understood only in the context of history.

One characteristic of Philippines society that has constantly served to dampen Philippines growth is the concentration of economic power in a few. It is this that has made it easy for Marcos to deliver Philippine banking, industrial and commercial life into the hands of his cronies. This reality is seen by every Filipino -- not only by the communist-minded who riles against the elite for his own reason. This is the all-encompassing reality that makes entrepreneurship an occupation far away from the dreams of the majority of Filipinos.

The start of really dramatic growth in all societies has been the transition from economy mainly of low paying, low-productivity rural employment to an economy that consists of a smaller rural part, which is highly productive, plus a larger part which is high in industrial employment. The Philippines has not experienced this shift. Not during "golden years" of the 50's and early 60's, not during the Marcos regime, and not yet now. In the past 20 years, a World Bank report says the share of urban labor in the total Philippines output has increased only by 3 percent. Malaysia, all of which including Kuala Lumpur was like a Philippine province in the 1950s, experienced an increase of 27 percent. South Korea increased by 27 percent.

This underscores the fact that in the Philippines the population of middle income earners—people who are in the middle between the poor farmers and the minimum wage factory workers on one hand and the urban rich (in whose ranks belong the Filipino billionaires who appear in the Fortune list as well as the professionals and entrepreneurs who earn about US$2,000 a month) on the other -- is negligible. The absence of a large population of middle-income earners results in what has been called a dual-economy society in which the majority of the people are just above the poverty line or in fact below it, while a very small minority--the elite which ridiculously include even those who have sons and daughters earning good pay in Saudi Arabia,

Singapore, Hong Kong, Britain or the USA and Canada-- control the economy. These elite make up less than 10% of the population.

Now within these elite there is an even sharper dichotomy.

The higher level of this, the so-called A&B economic bracket, makes up only less than one percent of the total population. So that you can count the 9 percent of this elite as the true middle class.

This one percent, cream of the elite, controls the country's economic life. They are the oligopoly. They own the firms that control every aspect of the banking industry, commerce, tourism, import and export, retail trade, entertainment, movies and even distribution of Philippines-made records and cassettes. The majority of men and women in national politics and of those who makeup the upper echelons of government belong to the tinniest of the upper crust.

Old Wine, Late Bloom

A survey has shown that of the 1000 Philippine firms that control the economic life, the top four of the 1000 have a concentration ratio of 70%. This means that the top four Philippine firms control 70% of the businesses in their field. Even Indonesia, which is outrightly less democratic that the Philippines and reputedly more corrupt, has a comparable concentration ratio of only 56%. Other countries such as South Korea shows 62%, while Mexico, Chile and Brazil are at about 50%.

No wonder small and medium-size-firms-- which are common in Japan, Korea, Taiwan, Hong Kong and

Singapore--hardly exist in the Philippines. These firms are very important for balanced social and economic development, for these are in fact the subcontractor firms, small companies that, for instance in Japan, contribute their share in making headlights, door handles, radios, upholstery, etc. to the making of the Toyota Camry sold by the American dealers in USA.

In the Philippines, the small firms cannot avail themselves of loans from the banks. The banks exist to serve the industrial and commercial interests of their owners, not of their depositors or small entrepreneurial clients.

Without a healthy component of middle-income earners consisting of the entrepreneurs and employees of these small firms, the Philippines will find it hard to advance to the next stage our competitive neighbors are now in. For it is the presence and strength of this middle group that prevents government from passing laws that benefit only the elite or bending the laws and trade rules and regulations in favor of the elite. In the Philippines, "nationalistic" laws have been passed to protect weak elite firms in the guise of promoting business and trade for everybody. To laws passed to liberalize trade, exceptions were made exempting elite-owned companies and industries.

It is also these elites who had in fact collaborated with all forms of foreign occupation or threat as long as their own specific interests were safeguarded. This was the case during the Spanish regime, the American colonial period and the post-colonial era.

PART II: CONSCIOUSNESS, SPIRIT AND VISION

To a degree, less or more, all the above factors discussed so far have impacted our social economic life.

But there remain three factors which I consider crucial.

NATIONAL CONSCIOUSNESS

First is our lack of well-formed national consciousness, which prevents us as a people from having commonly shared aspirations, commonly held ambitions--to foster national prosperity.

We are a country of many islands and our mentality and attitudes reflect that geography. We have scarcely progressed from the **Barangay** mentality or mentality of the tribe. Our nation has its beginning when the ten datus from the Indo-Malaysian region came to our shores. The boats they sailed on were called *Barangay* and so were the communities they established. Essentially, these individual communities remained separate and became self-contained kingdoms. They did not coalesce for any collective effort or endeavor.

Today, we still largely think of ourselves as Tagalogs, Ilocanos, Pangasinenses, Cebuanos or Ilonggos, etc. Just look at the proliferation of Filipino organizations based on geographic origin here in the United States.

And this splinterization is not limited to provincial groupings; some are subdivided further into towns, or for that matter, into the smallest barrios! While this myriad of associations does serve the networking aims of particular individuals, they rarely collaborate with one another as effective organizations uniting their members for some common noble projects or tasks.

We are a people who have not yet sufficiently come together. And as such, the habit of thinking, much less of getting our act together, for what is good for the larger society escapes us. We find it so difficult to put the interest of the nation above our petty individual interests.

There is even a darker side to this whole thing. I refer to the oft-quoted "crab mentality" of the Filipinos.

Instead of feeling proud and glory in the high achievements of some of our **kababayans,** we tend to pull them down, discredit them. We ingratiate ourselves to those who hold the lever of power just to pull down someone of our own who happens to be above us.

A shade lighter to this dark nature is our incapacity to trust anyone outside our family or clan. Truly, we still have the mentality of the tribe. This is best illustrated in some business ventures in which some people invest their money. In a number of instances somebody absconds with the money. And the business collapses.

Somebody always wants to make a fast buck. Do you remember the financial debacle in California involving a car dealership? How about that investment lady in New York who was into oil drilling? She too ran away with the money and is reported living "happily ever after" somewhere in Europe, perhaps buying herself into a countess title. Her investors were left holding the bag minus the money. It is my understanding that in some cultures, such as the Japanese, Chinese and Koreans, a deal could be made by mere handshake and is honored.

Filipinos would go through the whole trouble of putting it all in writing, such as a contract, a constitution and by-laws, but is worth less than the paper it is written on; sooner or later someone will run away with the money.

If we have a stronger sense of nationhood, and therefore a sense of our common destiny and aspirations as a people, we would be less prone to giving in to these base tendencies and are more likely to pull ourselves together.

As a people we have very little to show, and therefore command very little respect, although it is obvious that within our race are outstanding individuals who have made a name for themselves in their chosen fields here and other parts of the world.

And the reason for this is that we have constantly refused to act on the truism that the whole is more than the sum of its parts.

Nation building, such as getting our economy out of the third-world poor status, takes more than individual efforts and successes. It requires a common purpose to which one works in concert with others to achieve.

How do we arrive at a common purpose? By a deeper sense of who we are, a **national consciousness.**

And this can be acquired only by digging into our history and culture.

The degree of ignorance of most Filipinos about their history and culture is appalling. The miss-education of the Filipinos, to quote Filipino historian Renato Constantino, must be rectified so that we and the younger generations will develop a greater consciousness of our self-worth as a nation. Then we can have pride in being Filipinos.

Lacking in national consciousness, national pride, national purpose and common aspirations, we are vulnerable to external pressures and fail to identify and protect our national interest, or worse, to confuse – naively and sometimes disastrously – our national interests with that of another country.

Let me elaborate:

The sad experience of the Philippines vis-à-vis the World Bank is an example of how the Philippine elites--which control business, finance, industry and government--have allowed damage to happen to the nation.

The World Bank's purpose is to promote free global trade and commerce. It lends money to countries in the context of that over-arching objective. It is supported with funds from the United States and Western Europe, because global free trade is the lifeblood of these countries which make products for exports to the world.

Small countries such as the Philippines must be wise in dealing with such institutions. When what the World Bank wants the Philippines to do is good for the Philippines as well as for the developed countries then the Philippines should agree to implement it. If it does not serve the Philippines' interest but only the rich and powerful nations, then the Philippines should not agree. Or, if it's forced to agree because it is weak and it needs the loans from the rich countries and the World Bank like a beggar, it should only implement World Bank demands cleverly.

That's what Japan, Korea, Singapore, Malaysia, Thailand and Taiwan – all the successful countries – did and still do. While the so-called tiger economies said "Yes, yes" and smiled to the World Bank, they did only what was good for themselves.

In the 1960s, the World Bank demanded that the Philippines devalue the Philippine peso. In those days a strong peso was an important important factor for our industrialization drive; our infant industries needed to import capital goods and raw materials to keep them going. The devaluation of the peso, along with the lifting of import and exchange controls, was a severe blow to our burgeoning industries.

In 1981, when the Marcos regime decided on a rather good policy to establish 11 basic industries in the Philippines, the World Bank opposed it. The policy, if implemented, would have (unless of course Marcos cronies made a mess of the whole thing) assured the Philippines of its own petrochemical, fertilizer and plastic supplies; it would have developed an indigenous steel industry, instead of it being dependent on other countries for steel imports, an anomalous situation since the Philippines is a major exporter of iron ore, the raw material for steel. Under World Bank pressure, these 11 industrial projects were scuttled by the Marcos regime.

In 1992, the World Bank report on the Philippines said, among other ironic things, that the fundamental reason the Philippine economy had been sluggish was that it did not have its own petrochemical, steel, fertilizer and various basic industries. The World Bank report even cited how Thailand, poorer that the Philippines two decades ago, had now become richer and more self-reliant because it built its own basic industries.

Milk is more expensive in the Philippines that elsewhere because we have no tin, plastics and cardboards. Hangers and clothesline are expensive because we have no indigenous plastic resin plants. Even our exports are more expensive that those from other Third World countries because we have to import plastic packaging materials. If we had our own steel industry we could, like Malaysia, make our own cars or trucks with a Japanese or American partner. Now we are only assembling cars. Whereas in colonial times, we were exporting our extractive products, natural resources, and few primary primary produce such as abaca, copra, sugar, now with the "assembly" industry we are only "exporting" our labor, not our processed, creative or innovative, high value-added products

It is not too late to correct the situation. We still must build these basic industries, even if only to make sure our own people get milk, medicines, hangers, clothes and clotheslines cheaper.

CULTURE & TRADITION
OF ENTERPRENEURSHIP

Not knowing who and what we are, it is not surprising we are found wanting in the spirit of enterprise.

For to embark in the "uncharted sea" takes a good deal of self-worth and courage.

The second reason for our laggard economic performance vis-à-vis our fellow East Asians is our lack of culture and tradition of entrepreneurs. We do have entrepreneurs and businessmen. But they aren't yet in sufficient numbers as to permeate and impact significantly our national life. Our entrepreneurs do not captivate the hearts and minds of the people like the politicians – and actors and actresses – do. They are not role models the way actors, actresses and politicians are. They're not normally held up as cultural icons. We do not yet breathe and live entrepreneurship. It doesn't yet come to us as second nature. That is what is meant by culture of entrepreneurship which, if sustained long enough, gives a people a tradition of entrepreneurship.

At the most fundamental level, entrepreneurship is about individual effort, initiative, resourcefulness, creativity, insight, foresight and risk-taking.

Yet it would be a mistake to conceive of it as an all or nothing principle, as something that you either have or you don't. The qualities that make for entrepreneurial skills are learned. Entrepreneurs are not born, but made. Of course, there are a few gifted individuals who tower for above the crowd, such as Bill Gates, Jobs, Krocs, etc. But these are not the people we're talking about. These are the exceptions that prove the rule, just as there are exceptions in other fields of endeavors. For the vast majority of entrepreneurs, they sweat it out, they study, and they work hard, make mistakes and learn from their mistakes.

And embarking on this learning curve and ascending it is fostered and nurtured by what I call a culture and tradition of entrepreneurship. One strives to learn the basics, or even the nuances and subtleties of a business, but one is encouraged, sustained and inspired in the endeavor by its culture.

Along the way, one gains the confidence, the poise to move on and scale greater heights. For entrepreneurship is also a game of snowballing confidence like any aspect of life. It builds upon one success over another, and a series of successes that exceed the moments of failure.

The making of an entrepreneur is not unlike the making of a doctor. When you finish medical school you may have all the knowledge in the world about medical science but you are not yet a doctor; you have to go through rigorous internship, residency, and maybe fellowship. You breathe, sleep and eat medicine. You immerse yourself in its science as much as in its culture. In the process you learn the fine points of diagnosis and the treatment of diseases. At the same time you learn about human nature and how to relate with other people effectively, which is as important in your success or failure as a doctor as it is an entrepreneur doing business.

What is interesting to note is that once a beachhead is made in a certain field of endeavor, it becomes easier for others to follow. That's why in many families you see a family of lawyers, accountants and engineers.

That is because the experience of the preceding members of the family provides the necessary environment and confidence for the succeeding generations to go to the same field.

The same is true in business – and entrepreneurship.

We Filipinos do not yet have a culture of entrepreneurship. It is not that we are capable of it. It is simply we have not yet developed the necessary environment, practices and attitudes towards it. It is about time we embark on this road.

How? Just by going into it. By giving due recognition to those people who have embarked on it and have succeeded. By creating incentive for business to thrive. By inculcating values that go into the making of entrepreneurs or businessmen. By imitating the Japanese, Chinese and Koreans.

There should be no shame in imitating. Look, the Japanese do it, the Koreans do it. The Chinese do it.

And look where they are.

We could build a culture of entrepreneurship. At first, it will be by force of will and deliberate effort, but later it will come to us as second nature.

In the words of Peter Drucker, the foremost guru of American Management, entrepreneurship is the key that will unlock the Twenty First Century. Indeed, it has already done so for the Japanese, the Chinese and the Koreans for the twentieth century. So it shall be for us Filipinos if we follow this path.

The Filipinos have demonstrated themselves to be capable managers of business enterprises, but have yet to be captains and owners of such enterprises of notable global reach. Only then will the Filipino be accorded the respect that he or she deserves.

Past Industrialization Drive: Revisited

Actually, for us Filipinos, it is not as if we're entirely ignorant of entrepreneurship. Something of a morphic resonance-- to borrow a phrase from Rupert Sheldrake's The Rebirth of Nature, a fantastic and fascinating book – from our not too distant past comes to mind. In the 1950s and early 1960s we embarked on industrialization and entrepreneurship. Under the impetus of import and exchange controls Filipinos entrepreneurs and businessmen started to build factories and to manufacture goods that formerly were imported, mainly from the United States. And very modestly we were beginning to export some goods to our Asian neighbors. It was during this period that the Philippines was experiencing unprecedented growth and Filipinos gaining confidence in themselves.

But this drive towards industrialization and entrepreneurship was short-lived. In the early 1960s, under the leadership of President Macapagal, the import and exchange controls were dismantled. And the peso was also devalued. As if these were not enough, restrictive monetary policies were also instituted. These virtually spelled the death knell of our infant industries.

There are those who argue that the industrialization we launched was nothing more than **another face of importation,** albeit a different one (this time we were importing capital goods and raw materials rather than consumer goods), because the importation per se became the business itself, becoming more dominant and lucrative than the industries it was supposed to serve.

With this industrialization drive, the Filipino businessmen/entrepreneur and exponent of economic nationalism (so-called nationalist) found uncommon alliance, with the former seeing it as an opportunity to pursue his economic interest and the latter seeing it as the chance to expand and extend the cause of nationalistic aspirations from the political to the economic realm.

The industrialization effort was import substitution in nature, oriented towards the domestic market. It was thought by some economist, **mostly free-market advocates,** to be shortsighted, because it could not have sustained itself were it not for the foreign exchange from other sources. It was consuming foreign exchange and practically earning or paying nothing for it. Foreign exchange earned from the export of primary products (such as sugar, abaca, and coconut) and extractive products (such as gold and copper) financed the importation of capital goods and raw material for our industries.

There was tremendous pressure on our foreign exchange reserve, giving rise to well publicized scandals.

Some took advantage of the differential between the exchange rate of the dollar and its value in the domestic market, putting more pressure in the dollar. The temptation for corruption was great. The apparent widespread corruption was one of the reasons (some say a pretext) for the lifting of the import and exchange controls.

It was also thought that during that period (import and exchange controls) the peso was overvalued, making our products--other than primary products and extractive produce--uncompetitive in the world market, thereby perpetuating the pattern of our export-- that of a colonial exporting nation.

Furthermore, import controls made higher prices for poor-quality domestic product because of lack of competition from outside. Our businessmen were charging as much as the market would bear.

And lacking any foreign competition in the domestic market, our businessmen became complacent, failed to innovate and improve the quality of their products thereby unable to compete even more in the world market.

As to the argument that it was during this period that the country was most prosperous, it was thought to be an illusion and contrived. As the counter-argument goes, you may look prosperous if you sell the family jewels (e.g. natural resources) or buy on credit or with inflated peso.

From another camp, this time from the **exponent of economic nationalism**, comes the criticism that the industrialization we embarked on was nothing more than assembly-type industrialization. They were dismissive, if not disdainful, of our efforts at the manufacture of shoes, garments and assembly of certain goods.

Their idea of real industrialization was along the so-called heavy industries, modeled after the Soviet Union and the Eastern-block countries.

The above points of view, from **the free-market advocates and from the economic nationalists**, are probably too harsh or extreme. The truth probably lies in somewhere in the middle.

As to the advocates of heavy industry model, they forget that the light industries are stepping stones for bigger things. They are part of the learning curve. Rarely are there gigantic and immediate breakthroughs in economic development, as in almost all fields of human endeavors. Even science is characterized by long and painstaking observation, experimentation and gathering of data before a major synthesis in terms of a theory is made. Incrementalism, rather than leapfrogging, is more the nature of things, including economic development. In any case, the heavy industry advocates have only to look at the collapse of their model. This is not to say that the basic industries are not important. But to put all our eggs in the basket of heavy industries is foolish. There should be some kind of balance between the light and heavy industries, a kind of complementarity, and a consideration of where you deploy or sell the products of those industries and how are they supported or promoted (e.g. government or private sector).

As to those who are overly critical of our industrialization efforts in the 1950s and early 1960s from the opposite camp, **the free-marketers**, it can be said that up until that time entrepreneurship was almost unknown notion, or was hardly perceptible in our national life.

We had to start somewhere. As an infant needs the nurturing and protection of his mother, so did our infant industries needed the protection of the government/state. It was not as if we were big boys and girls, much less adults, right from the start. It is not as if we could be industrialists or entrepreneurs overnight. Under the protective mantle of controls, the Filipinos were allowed to be born, and to grow, as businessmen and entrepreneurs into the realm of big business, hitherto largely unfamiliar to them, breaking away from the world of the small-scale **sari-sari** store, long the metaphor for Filipino business enterprise.

But you have to grow up and cannot be under the protection of "mama" forever. You have to come into your own sometime.

The question is often asked: Were the controls dismantled prematurely, preventing us from moving into the next stage of development and growth? Or were they long overdue stunting our maturation?

As I see it, it was not a question of premature dismantling or a case of it being long overdue. The problem was: **It was a failure of vision.** We failed to look beyond our noses. We cannot see beyond the horizon. We failed to formulate a parallel or complementary policy that was outward-looking. And this brings me to my last major point.

VISION AND THE GLOBAL MARKET

The third major reason is our failure to look for opportunities in the world market. Here we are talking about the lack of vision on the part of our national leaders – in business, industry, politics and intellectual life.

Our national leaders have failed to grasp the central idea that our national economy is only a minuscule part of the world economy (0.7%), and doing business with the world offers immeasurably far greater returns than doing business with the domestic market. [This is far from saying that the domestic economy doesn't count. A strong domestic economy can be the launching pad for competitive industry or industries – in the context of Michael Porter's formulation (in his book **Competitive Advantage**) – in the global market].

Our Asian neighbors have grasped that idea early on and have met head-on the challenges, and have seized the opportunities, in the global economy, and have sold to and bought from the world. We have largely chosen to sell to and buy from ourselves.

In my view this was/is a major cause for our economic stagnation, even retrogression. This was the crucial difference between our Asian neighbors who are so far ahead and us who have lagged so far behind. Our national economy is about 0.7 percent of the world economy which means: if we can sell to that market with quality and highly differentiated products, produced efficiently, commanding good or premium prices, we earn precious foreign exchange which not only lift our standard of living, but provides us with the necessary capital to fuel our economy, upgrade our factories and streamline our management technique, which will enable us to compete even more effectively in the world market.

It is export to world that made possible the economic miracle that is the Pacific Rim (exceptus). It is in this area that we have failed so miserably.

Because of our aborted entrepreneurial development, and hence, our industrialization, one gets the feeling that competition in the global scale is not something that enters the consciousness of the Filipinos. One even gets the impression that the word sends a chill down the spine of Filipinos. It is as if we have lost our nerve. Thus, we prefer to be secure – within ourselves, within our family, within clan or tribe; we are **seguritas** rather than risk-takers. This is the "Heritage of Smallness" that Nick Joaquin speaks of.

We have to break away from this mentality, from this culture. We have to break through our shell that contains us. We have to regain our confidence.

It was not until modern Japan, Taiwan, Singapore, Thailand and Korea discovered the world that they became the miracle economies they are today. Not until we go out into the world and sell to the world, **and stop contemplating our navel,** can we achieve prosperity for our people.

It is far better to export goods than export people. Goods may be thrown about, kicked around and all you get are damaged goods. You can always manufacture the same and not much harm is done. But when people are beaten, and virtually enslaved, or owned like pieces of property or made as sex objects, as what is obtaining now with many

Filipinos in many parts of the world, then something is fundamentally wrong. It cannot but hurt us individually and collectively as a people. We feel their pain, their anguish, their humiliation, and perhaps, even their rage. Our national pride takes a dive. Something is diminished in us individually and as a people. It hurts when someone (James Fallows) label us as "damaged culture," even if were true.

We have to redeem ourselves. We must not be afraid to compete in the world. We have seen the genius of our people, if only exemplified in the individual level. We have seen our doctors excel, our scientists and artists more than hold their own. Man for man we are equal to one and all. What we need is a culture of entrepreneurship springing from, founded on and built in, the context of our national consciousness, common destiny and common aspirations as a people, looking outward to the world for opportunities even as we look inward for the same.

As we edge nearer to the close of this century we see clearly the tragedy of our diaspora. We have been scattered to all corners of the world. For many of us, especially those who have come to the United States, we have found self-realization, the good life, and the fulfillment of our dreams. For some, unfortunately, they have found only misery, abuse and violence in parts of the world where people are less tolerant and welcoming towards immigrants. We cannot help but empathized with their condition.

Our diaspora, whether it has brought us personal or individual prosperity or misery, has opened, or should open, our eyes to the world, the world of opportunities in terms of trade, not as places to export our people (like goods).

Already, the younger generation of Filipinos, better educated than their forebears and who have seen the world, are beginning to have a world view. Even our usually complacent business leaders are seeing the light.

Up until recently, San Miguel Brewery had been content to do business in the Philippines only; now it's venturing into Australia and other Asian countries. One wishes that it would have the boldness of spirit-- like

Honda and Hyundai, much smaller companies than San Miguel in the 60s, but now global players—to cross the

Atlantic and make its presence in America or Europe with more innovative products or joint-venture projects in these parts of the world.

Our multi-millionaire/billionaire Filipino-Chinese businessmen are, finally, getting more aggressive globally, catching up with their Chinese counterparts in other Asian countries such Malaysia, Singapore, Taiwan, and Hong Kong, whose business all over the world contributed mightily to the prosperity of their nations.

The Zobel-Ayalas--like ther Filipino-Chinese business moguls who had seemed merely content of capturing the dollar remittances of OFWs (which amounts to about $ 10 B annually)--are similarly making tentative moves to be engaged in global trade.

Jollibee has ventured in California, although its area of operations are largely confined to Filipino communities in that state. But such small steps are welcome, if only as confidence builders.

The advances in telecommunications and travel are making the world indeed a smaller place. This will only accelerate our interaction and integration with the world economy, making us see opportunities where they exist, and establish a niche in them, and exploit our competitive advantage to our benefit.

In the words of Nick Joaquin, we as a people are in the process of becoming. If that be the case, we are open to possibilities. We may yet see a keener sense of national consciousness, common destiny and shared aspirations.

Old Wine, Late Bloom

Paradoxically, I believe that the very advances in communications and travel technologies that have contracted the world and have brought people closer together are the very same instruments that will sharpen our national consciousness and identity, infuse us with the spirit of enterprise and entrepreneurship and expand our world view-- the key ingredients, in my opinion, for our economic development.

Let us be encouraged by a fact that has not been given much attention. In 1983, the World Bank report classified the Philippines as a "Newly Industrialized Country." Only the chaos of Aquino assassination pushed us back to the bottom.

I have no doubt in my mind that we can rise above our present condition. After all, in spite of our character deficiencies (and what people don't have some flaws!), in spite of our own folly and self-destructive tendencies, in spite of monstrous natural disasters, such as Mt. Pinatubo, in spite of World War II that reduced our country to a rubble, we have demonstrated a remarkable degree of resiliency. We have survived! Now the task before us is not only to show that we can survive, but thrive as a people.

7
Primary Care, Philippines

Dateline: Feb. 6, 2014

Philippine Healthcare: An Overview

1) Under recent and present conditions, given the Philippine situation with its exploding population, now close to 100 million, an economy that's improving, but far from solidly strong as its Asian neighbors, a governance that's permeated with corruption, providing adequate basic health and medical care to the vast majority of our people is an enormous challenge.

2) There have been some improvements in terms of health indices such as maternal and infant mortality rates (!); new programs to control TB put in place; modest efforts at upgrading the government provincial hospitals initiated; programs to develop the management skills of some doctors (not traditionally in the curriculum of med education) are on-going (2); more doctors are being deployed to the towns and municipalities, including towns in the far-flung places in the Philippines (3); a government-sponsored health insurance (PhilHealth) (4) now cover about 85% of Filipinos (at least in paper), a not insignificant segment of which is exempted recently from balance-billing (although majority of Filipinos still spend about 48 % of the medical bill from their pockets), the outflow of Filipino doctors and other health providers to other countries have considerably slowed down -- still the goal of providing health and basic medical care to the great majority of the our people remains elusive.

A Tale of Two Health Systems

3) In major cities in the Philippines, especially in Metro Manila, you have a number of modern hospitals where one gets the best of care comparable to anything in the world; these modern hospitals are staffed by doctors trained locally

and most obtained advanced training from all over the world, especially from the US; they are conversant with modern technology, equipment, and gadgets. The doctors in these medical centers are capable of doing the latest surgical and medical procedures such as by-pass heart surgery, coronary artery stenting, vascular surgery of any kind, neurosurgical interventions; plastic or cosmetic surgery of any kind, orthopedic procedures including hip and knee replacements, spine surgery; latest gastrointestinal surgical procedure and diagnostic methods, etc. In fact, for nearly any kind of surgical and medical diagnostic and therapeutic modalities, one does not go abroad; as a matter of fact, we have a modest number of medical tourists who seek their care in the Philippines; we're slowly being competitive with other Asian countries in this respect. Given further support by the government and far better marketing, the Philippines should become the destination for more medical tourists, given the fact that apart from the excellent medical care they receive, we continue to develop tourist experiences and amenities to enhance their stay in the country. It's generally not known that our National Kidney and Transplant Institute is internationally renowned for kidney transplantation for many years now and its clients come from all over the world.

4) But the costs of these high-tech medicine and surgical procedures are expensive, far beyond the reach of most Filipinos. This is true in the urban areas and more acutely, in fact, not available in most instances in the provinces. Although technically 85% of Filipinos are now covered with government health insurance, **PhilHealth,** the out- of- pocket expenses for most patients are nothing less than prohibitive; the no-balance billing is very much limited to the most indigent of patients only (5). Moreover, the number of participating and accredited doctors, other health providers, hospitals and other health institutions are not yet extensive enough for most Filipinos to access them with their PhilHealth coverage. (6)Thus, it remains a question of access for them. When you add on the cost of medicines and medical supplies then you're talking of medical bills far beyond the financial resources of ordinary Filipinos, especially for those in extreme poverty; the generic medicines

help, but even then the cost of medical care is a steep mountain to climb.

Manpower

5) The above situation is true for both urban and rural areas, much more so in the latter. The health system (a chain of provincial/city hospitals, rural health units, barangay heath units) in the provinces was severely at risk in terms of manpower 5-7 years ago; there was tremendous exodus of doctors from the Philippines. It was not unusual then for even heads of departments changing careers, even for those who had spent 15-20 years of career in medicine, taking nursing courses just so they could could go abroad to work as nurses. That was at the height of demand for nurses abroad, especially from North America and Europe. Nursing Schools proliferated and graduated excessive number of nurses. Only the nosedive of the world economy slowed down the tide of health provider exodus. Suddenly the demand from Western and developed countries slowed down to a trickle. Then we faced the opposite problem: excess of unemployed nurses and other health professionals.

Brick & Mortars; Equipments & Supplies

6) The delivery of health care in the provinces has been hampered by other factors. For one thing the brick and mortar assets (buildings) have not been maintained and constructions of new ones have not kept pace with the exploding population. Many if not most have not been upgraded or replaced. Support personnel are inadequate. Supplies are chronically short. For many cases, patients are provided prescriptions by doctors to buy the needed medicines and supplies from outside the hospitals. The rural health units are a pale comparison of themselves in the early 60s, many of them now are not functional due to unmaintained structures, lack of personnel and supplies. There are now so called **barangay health units**, not doing any better than the old rural health units, besides being at an early stage of implementation. How these differ in function with the rural health units, I don't know; perhaps, this is an

effort to bring services closer to the people and consolidate the **other functions** of barangay units with health and medical issues, making more efficient use of the office assets of the barangay units.

7) Most of the health facilities (hospitals, clinics laboratories) in the provinces and

Municipalities are in private hands (7). Generally one cannot be admitted to these Places or obtain their services without first making a deposit or paying in cash up front. If a patient is admitted at all, the patient is charged on a daily basis and, if he/she can't, she's under undue pressure to be discharged whether he/she is fully recovered or not. In the most dire circumstances, almost at the point of dying, a patient is admitted to stabilize him/her; the patient is either discharged to a public hospital or home once the he/she is somewhat stabilized.

8) The public hospitals in the provinces or municipality are overflowing with patients, many of them spilling over into the corridors. Many are prematurely sent home to make room for new patients, quickly given a prescription, given false, perfunctory reassurance at times, and asked to return the next day or in a few days.

Local Government Code, Local Government Units (LGU) & the Department of Health

9) The devolution of powers to Local Government Units (LGU), consistent with the intention of making local officials more directly responsible and accountable to the people ironically enough has compounded the delivery of health care to the people in the province and municipalities. (8) The Department of Health (DOH) has the overall governance of health policy and programs in the country. It still supervises the running and funding of the provincial hospitals. But below that level, at the city and municipal level, they are effectively under the control and responsibility of the city and municipal officials. Undoubtedly many of these officials know what they are doing with the

help and guidance of their medical staff; but some probably do not have the slightest idea of how to run the health side of their duties.

10) An equally important issue is that some municipalities or cities have funds to run these health institutions (9), but the poorer municipalities do not the have resources, which means even less or even lack of provision of care. Sometimes these health institutions are run as small fiefdoms of local politicians, on a patronage system, from staffing to dispensing of supplies and drugs, even making arbitrary decisions on who'll get charity care or not.

11) The operational relationships of the DOH and the LGU are not yet well defined and are works in progress; these act as speed bumps to the proper, effective, efficient and economical delivery of services to the people.

Major Diseases: Acute Causes

12) The major diseases in the Philippines are still acute respiratory and gastrointestinal ones: pneumonia, bronchitis, asthma, bronchiolitis, acute gastroenteritis, dengue, TB, parasitic diseases (10). Maternal and infant mortality rates have substantially declined (11), but by the standards of more affluent neighboring countries we're still lagging far behind. HIV/AID programs are existent , but not widespread. Drug addiction among the young is a problem, and drug trafficking is apparently common in the country.

13) These diseases are very much amenable to treatment and intervention. The do not require high-tech, high cost medical intervention and manageable at the level of the common doctor and hospitals. But the problem is again access to health or medical care delayed or denied due to financial constraints. Many of these usual diseases end up going to over overcrowded municipal and provincial hospitals where admissions are difficult; many patients are perfunctorily evaluated, given prescriptions, which the family could not afford, or buying the required medicines for as few as a couple of days, not enough to treat or cure the disease. As I

said there are private hospitals or facilities, but the cost of admission or care is prohibitive or nearly prohibitive.

Chronic Medical Diseases

14) What is getting increasingly worrisome is the emergence and persistence of non-communicable, chronic diseases (11). They were not unknown during our time. These diseases such as hypertension, diabetes, stroke, coronary artery disease, heart failure, hyperlipidemia, renal failure, asthma, chronic bronchitis, emphysema and drug multi-drug resistant TB have become prevalent. These are now the major diseases that negatively impact the health of many Filipinos, which, because of their chronicity are expensive to treat and are a tremendous burden on a family's financial resources. Not infrequently, the patients, for financial reasons, simply stop taking medications, assuming a fatalistic attitude of "bahala na." In the meantime, the disease progresses with serious complications, which at this point may no longer be amenable to easy control and far more expensive to treat. A good example is somebody with hypertension which is cheap and very easy to treat; but if the patient takes it for granted, it surely and slowly destroy his kidney or impairing his heart function; in time he develops heart failure, heart beat irregularity and/or kidney failure; at this point the cost of treatment skyrockets, practically unaffordable for the patient or family.

15) In the past, in our time, most of these chronic diseases were not common, but now because of the drastic changes in our diet (high fat, high sugar, increased calories) it's mind boggling how common they are. When I was an intern at PGH in 1968-1969, I personally saw **only four cases** of diabetes in one year, only one of whom had what we call diabetes ketoacidosis. Now diabetes is so common locally and world-wide. Diabetes is an expensive disease to treat; oftentimes you have to employ a combination of two or three drugs; it's the number one cause of renal failure, necessitating dialysis, of blindness in the form of retinopathy and glaucoma, and major contributory factor in peripheral artery disease, which may require vascular reconstructive

surgery or amputation of the leg or foot. Usually the co-morbidities such as hypertension, high cholesterol are major factors for heart problems such as heart failure, coronary artery disease (blockage of heart artery), necessitating multiple drugs, and on many occasions requiring expensive diagnostic procedures or intervention and treatment such as angioplasty, stenting or by-pass surgery, all too far expensive for most Filipinos, oftentimes really beyond their reach, thus foregoing treatment and thereby die or get disabled prematurely.

16) But if these conditions are dealt early on, most of these complications are preventable and people live longer, productive lives. With effective primary care system most of these diseases can be effectively under control. With extensive health education program on lifestyle changes--- on diet, smoke cessation, exercise--most of them can be prevented and brought under control with the least cost.

17) For a country with limited resources and large population, the only way to deliver adequate and affordable health and medical care to the people, the only way to go is to develop a good and efficient **primary care system.** By a system we mean a systematic inventory of our resources, manpower and otherwise, assessment of the main medical challenges facing our people, addressing and deploying our resources efficiently and effectively. By primary and preventive we mean addressing the problems at their earliest clinical stage, or preventing them or adopting public health measures (e.g., potable water, sanitation, immunization, mosquito net, efficient sewage system) for the common diseases besetting our people.

18) As I previously alluded to, the ideal situation is for the patient to first go to his/her primary care physician, then upon the discretion of his/her doctor referred to a specialist, or may request that he/she be referred to a specialist with a brief note or pertinent info why the patient is being referred. This provides a communication tool for both doctors or health providers, to provide the doctors info as to the current

problems/ medication of the patient as well as previous medical problem that may be relevant to the current one.

Local Government Units (LGU) & DOH

19) The system has to be highly organized and coordinated. For us in the Philippines, apart from the problems already cited above, this poses a special challenge because of the bifurcation of authority and responsibility between the DOH and the LGU. Administration of such an enterprise is enormous. Lines of authority, and responsibility can be confusing and when it comes to funding it becomes even more problematic; the matter could become a Ping-Pong ball.

PhiHealth

20) With the institution of **PhilHealth,** although still limited in the amount it can reimburse providers for their services, the mechanism is at least in place for funding for services; this can be further fine-tuned and expanded as our economy continues to improve and new sources of funding are found such as the anticipated sin tax revenue. This government health-sponsored health insurance is supplemented in a small degree with private health insurances

Single-Payer System

21) As presently configured the healthcare system in thePhilippines is effectively a one-payer system mainly through **PhilHealth** (12), with a minuscule private sector insurance. But health and medical services are delivered through a combination of public and private institutions and facilities (13). In my view this should remain as the template for health and medical care in the Philippines, more along the model of the European health systems and other developed nations in the world in terms of payment mechanism. In these nations, although hospitals, health facilities and institutions and health providers are compensated by and through govt mechanism, allowed adequate compensation, the **profit**

motive, although not altogether squelched, are kept at modest to the minimum level. In other words, their health care system is not driven by maximization of return on investment or greed, as generally practiced by US corporations that form part of the the whole medical-health industrial complex, accounting largely for the far higher cost of health and medical care in the US with mediocre results as measured by regular health indexes. The Philippines, being a third world or developing country cannot afford this kind of system and still deliver adequate services to its people.

22) Health and medical care are matters of human rights, and should not be subject to the free reign of the market; sure, some degree of profit making should be allowed but firmly regulated and within or below a certain ceiling. It should not definitely drive the system like many regular businesses. In the health care industry, there is a tremendous plasticity of demand and it's so easy to justify doing one more test after another even when the benefits accruing to additional tests are diminishing; moreover, with more expensive tests, generally speaking the risks of the procedures increase and complications escalate. Not a few doctors would push the envelope on doing one more additional test solely for pecuniary reasons, not for valid medical reason or *evidence-based medicine,* where the result will not change the manner of treatment anyway.

Drugs: The cost of medicines is the biggest barrier toward better health

23) The cost of medicines in the Philippines constitutes about 49% of the TOTAL healthcare expenditures in the country. Brand-named drugs are 3X -35X higher in the Philippines than for the same drugs in India and some other Asian countries. With a population now close to 100 million Filipinos and health indices showing our country lagging behind other countries, that is, more our people are sick and sicker than other peoples, the market for drugs, including brand-named drugs, is huge.

24) Medicines, unaffordable to vast majority of our people, have become a major determinant of health. Something is seriously and fundamentally wrong. The prices of medicines are likely being manipulated. Aggressive advertising and freebies given to physicians incentivize physicians to prescribe the more expensive brand name drugs.

What happens is that drug companies identify target doctors in good market areas such cities and big towns and lobby them heavily. They provide them with outrageous perks (e.g., all-expenses paid trips to Hong Kong. Paris, London, Singapore, Japan, NYC, Toronto plus spending money, car services, gifts, etc.). These are not free lunches. In the end, it's the patients who pay for all these expenses: the drugs reps put the pressure, subtle or otherwise, on the target doctors and the latter of course oblige, if they want to have another trip to, say, Sao Palo.

25) Even generic drugs are more expensive in the Philippine than in certain other Asian countries. When the generic drug law was enacted, a preferential treatment was given to India, and other countries producing generic drugs were excluded. This uncompetitive practice does not work in favor of the consumers.

26) Moreover, under the generic law, it seemed that there have not been sufficient incentives given to our local manufacturers to keep the cost of drugs down.

27) It's about time that our public officials conduct an investigation into the anomalous practices of drug companies, local or foreign. The leaders of the Philippine Medical Association should address this matter and do something about it. They should remind themselves that patients come first, not the perks of doctors that come from drug companies.

28) The generic drug law should be revisited, making sure that they buy generic drugs from other qualified producers from other countries. Programs should be developed, and incentives given to our local businessmen

and entrepreneurs, to build a national generic drug industry. Additionally, they should make sure that the distribution or marketing of drugs is more diverse, not controlled by one or two pharmacy chain,

to introduce more competition in the market to reduce the cost of medicines

Primary Healthcare System: Public Health & Preventive Care

29) In building or rebuilding of the primary care health system of the Philippines there are several component that need to be addressed:

a) The infrastructure of our provincial hospitals and the rural health units and barangay health units. With the tremendous growth of population, doubtless there needs to be expansion of existing structures and repair and upgrade of old ones (14).

b)   Providing with basic supplies and basic equipments (e.g. basic laboratory machines, x-ray machines, surgical suites, surgical instruments and supplies.)

c)   Manpower commensurate to the volume and needs of patients.

d) Furnishing of modern equipment such as CT Scan and more modern laboratory equipments capable of doing more sophisticated tests or procedures. These are all expensive and, needless to say, most hospitals cannot afford to have them. It is suggested that a consortium of hospitals pool their resources together, buy or lease the necessary equipments, maintain them, provide them with adequate personnel for 24/7 operation. The same consortium may opt to maintain a fleet of ambulance vehicles with which to transport patient from one facility to another for certain procedures

30) It is suggested that the development of a primary care health system should be decidedly basic and low tech.

By basic I mean the doctors and other healthcare providers should put more emphasis on **public health measures** and **preventive care** and should have the capability to manage simple acute and chronic diseases, including immunization, prenatal care, screening for hypertension, diabetes, TB screening, diagnosis and treatment, malnutrition evaluation, mosquito control, use of more mosquito net, smoking cessation program, expansion of sewage system, extension of the reach of potable water system, health education especially as this relate to diet, smoking, proper intake of medicines for chronic diseases, etc.

31) Having practiced medicine for 45 years I'd say that about 75 % of diseases are within the capabilities and competencies of primary care doctors to diagnose and treat those diseases cited; referral to specialty medicine is seldom needed. Ninety percent of the time I referred to a specialist was when I needed special procedures such as colonoscopy, upper intestinal endoscopy, bronchoscopy, nuclear exercise cardiac test, cardiac cath/angioplasty or stent and other specialized procedures such as an echo, EEG, EMG, NCS. I must have been one of the most conservative and cost-effective doctor in my use of high tech in my practice, and I could say confidently that the outcomes for my patients compared favorably if not better than most of my peers.

32) Many if not often the use of high-cost, high tech medicine is a way to by-pass the important but painstaking practice of medicine: taking a good history and doing a good physical exam; high tech procedures are also done for fear of litigation (defensive medicine) and not uncommonly as business gimmick, to augment one's income. For instance, one of the most abused procedures in medicine is the use of EKG. I used to see some patients (in their 30s. 40s) without any symptom or significant history pointing to heart ailment and on exam nothing to suggest any heart condition having been given an EKG, and even echo or stress tests, all very expensive for the patient, but lucrative for the doctor. In the Philippines it's not uncommon for some mid-level employees or executives of some companies or corporations, private or

public, to speak proudly that they underwent executive check-up; most of these people ore in their 30s, mid to late 40s with no symptoms or significant history and negative on exam. I'd say nearly 100 % of the results of executive check up for this age group are negative. But one senses that the patient no only felt good, reassured, privileged, and perversely considered the executive check up as a status symbol. The set of tests done for the executive check up are mostly irrelevant and useless, and on occasions are even dangerous for they could lead to more involved tests that include some serious risks. These practices must be discouraged, if not condemned; health providers are taking advantage of patients' ignorance or because of asymmetrical access to relevant medical information.

Continuing Medical Education

33) Another component of the primary care health system should be a program of continuing education. It needs hardly emphasizing that there is an explosion of new knowledge and technology in medicine. In order for the doctors to keep abreast with the advances in medicine there should be a program of continuing education; this can be organized at a municipal/city/provincial level, regional level or national level; other health providers should be provided the same.

Health Manpower Education: Foundational to Building a Primary Healthcare System

34) The healthcare system being proposed is a more inclusive one that addresses the vast majority of the health and medical needs of our people, one characterized by accessibility, affordability and quality.

35) To achieve this vision, 1) the educational programs of health and medical manpower must be tailored to the needs of our people, and 2) to make the necessary changes least disruptive of the current educational system thereby facilitating the adoption of the proposed model.

36} A good starting point is the assets we all already have in our nursing graduates.

Over the last decade or more we produced nurses far in excess of our national needs. The impetus for producing a good deal of nurses is the demand for nurses in other countries, notably the US and Europe and the Middle East. With the financial debacle in those countries and/or more restrictive immigration policies, the exodus of nurses came to a dead stop. At first glance this seems to a waste; on a second look, they are precious assets. Most of these nursing graduates have clinical experience; their training lends easily to staffing the rural health centers and barangay health units in the country. With a little more instructions and seminars they can be given more clinical responsibilities and be able diagnose and treat simple medical problems; public health courses could be added to their training and they'd be able to manage and run the same health units, if doctors are not available. Equip them with internet connectivity to allow them to communicate and consult with doctors in larger health units or centers and they should be able to do more.

37) The same could be said of mid-wives. I don't know how many mid-wives we graduate and what the number of mid-wives in practice is. I have feeling that their services are underutilized. You give them seminars on public health and common diseases, acute and chronic, and they'll be able to do more.

38) For medical education, private medical schools should be encouraged to produce more primary care physicians (general internal medicine, family practice, general pediatrics). Incentives can be given to them by the govt by partly reimbursing the clinical training of such physicians) or giving them some tax credit for their expenses on equipment and facilities. (I don't think CHED has the power to dictate the choice of postgraduate training of their graduates).

39) The PhilHealth also could encouraged people to go to primary care by increasing the remuneration for primary physicians' services. The intellectual challenges of primary

care are by no means less than those in the specialties or subspecialties. But nothing Surpasses the disincentive to primary care than the wide disparity of the remuneration of primary care as against specialist/subspecialist.

40) We need medical clinical integration and administrative coordination of care that could easily and capably assumed by primary care physicians as much as the specialized skills and knowledge of specialists. Most doctors who go into specialties have general medicine/general pediatric background, but over the course of time, they lose the skills and knowledge in those general fields to see the "big picture," and simply concentrate on their specialties; the more they do so, the more the attrition in their general knowledge and skills and the less confident they are. Thus, we see the fragmentation of care, where one specialist is hardly communicating with other specialist or entirely ignorant of what other specialists are doing to the patient, including medications which could be at cross purposes with each other or adversely interacting. I submit, a fairly competent general internist or general pediatrician is in a better to position see the "big picture."

UPCM, Health Sciences Center, & Primary Care

41) The University of the Philippines was established to provide a high quality of higher education in the country; to lead in and be the anchor for the educational, intellectual economic and political development of the country; to produce its leaders. The UPCM, a major component of the UP system, has been mandated to produce great doctors in the country and to lead in the delivery of quality healthcare for the Filipino people. In exchange for this privilege the government underwrites their education at taxpayers' expense.

42) The University was meant to draw from the brightest pool of students across ALL socio-economic levels from all over the Philippines. The reality, however, is UP has become the haven of a substantial number, if not majority, of the socio- economic political elites of Philippine

society.

43) The fact is during our time at UP in the late 50s and 60s UP was an elite school in more than academic sense. True there were good number of students coming from middle and lower classes of of society, but UP effectively was where the sons and daughters of the socio-economic-political elites of the nation converged. Affluent families sent their kids to the elite private sectarian or non-sectarian grammar and high schools, but once they graduate from those elite schools they were sent to UP where they (parents) knew their children would get a great education at the fraction of the cost if they had sent their kids to the private elite colleges or universities, in effect displacing the students--equally talented and academically qualified--that would have come from the middle or lower economic classes of society.

44) This was where the socio-economic-political elites of the nation began to perpetuate themselves...in the best institution of higher education in the country at taxpayers' expense to the disadvantage the of those coming from lower rung of the socio-economic strata. These students had the advantage right from the start by virtue of their superior basic education (elementary and high school) compared with those who came from the lower the socio-economic ladder. Their superior elementary and high school education gave them a head start at UP. Needless to say, they dominated the entrance exam for or admission to UP.

An important innovation at UP: the rationalization of tuition at UP, whereby tuition fee was based on a graduated scale, depending upon a family's income or wealth; those who come from rich or affluent families pay the full tuition fee, and those who come from the lower socio-economic classes, pay a corresponding lower fees. If the students come from the creme de la creme of the of the batch of student enrolles, extremely bright, he/she is given full academic scholarship and may even have a stipend. If the program was even half implemented it would have at least largely leveled the playing field.

45) However, I don't know how effectively this was implemented, knowing how many people in the country hide (corruption being so pervasive) hide their assets and income. If the basis was mainly on personal income tax, the record would have been dismal, for many of the people "doctored" their income tax. If memory serves me right the BIR has a collection rate of less than 20%. This means that even with the rationalization of tuition fee at UP, the compliance rate is quite low; *maraming nakakalusot pa rin, circumventing* the system.

46) The reason I brought this up is that from some of the information I gathered at UPCM, many if not majority admitted come from the elite schools of the country like Ateneo, La Salle, elite girls schools. I'm confident that majority if not most of these students are motivated by the best of ideals and intentions, compassion for their fellow human beings, especially earlier in their schooling, training or career. However, wittingly or unwittingly, this skewed spectrum of students engenders a kind of mindset, a mindset more focused on the kind of people and conditions they've been exposed to; it's not that they don't care about people from the lower socioeconomic classes; it's more like "out of sight, of out of mind," sort of diverted attention or inattentiveness to the general social-economic-political milieu they live in.

47) I think it's for this reason that for some if not many graduates of UP (I cannot speak about private medical schools graduates) their social awareness is attenuated. Very few people think or talk about practicing among the common people; they dream of practicing in the big cities in the "cathedrals" of modern medicine, where their clientele are far more affluent and can afford their fees, or go abroad for greener pastures.

48) If we have to build a health system that is truly geared toward serving the needs of the common people and

more equitable system, the govt should develop a program that should rectify this imbalance. All things being equal, some more slots should be given to those who come from the middle class or poorer sector of society. It is this segment of students who could more easily identify with that segment of society where they come from and thereby be more sensitive advocates for their natural constituents' needs. This is not to say that those who come from the elite segment of society are lacking in compassion or capacity for empathy with the poor, but many are less than attentive or attuned to them because of the milieu they move around is not dissimilar to their lifestyle to they are accustomed.

Satellite Health Sciences Colleges and Schools

49) The UP System is getting more sensitive to this issue, both as a matter of justice and practical matter with respect to building up a primary care system. In particular, the UPCM has been building satellite health science colleges in the Philippines. It envisioned three such schools, one in Mindanao, one in Visayas and one in Cordillera region. The one in the Visayas is located in Palo, Leyte and is already operational. It offers medical degree, nursing course, pharmacy, and midwifery. The medical school is geared toward producing primary care physicians and students are recruited from the same province or region. Their education is subsidized by the government, coursed through UPCM. Some medical students who are highly motivated and demonstrate adequate and superior performance recommended to UPCM (Manila) for more specialized training.

50) Part of the contract of the students with the school is for them to return to their communities and hopefully plant their roots their for the rest of their professional career; but of course, this is just a hope but the actual contract for how long they have to stay in their communities or region to pay back what the government spent for them, I do not know. The other locations are for satellite colleges are still on the drawing board. The primary health system will be boosted if these satellite schools come to fruition or even increased.

51) Further, the UPCM (Manila), recognizing that it's the people's money that is underwriting the education of medical students and that most of the graduates after finishing go abroad, has adopted a new policy for admitting students: to stay in the country for a number of years (equal to the number of years they studied in the college) to render service to the people before they could go abroad; otherwise, if they want to leave the country right after graduation, they have to reimburse the college for their full tuition fee. This seems to be a drastic change, but it seems only fair for the Filipino people who after all are the ones who underwrite their medical education. I think this policy has been in effect now for a couple of years. Alternatively, the student may pursue graduate studies on his own expense if he does not opt to do service work after graduation.

It needs emphasizing that the building of a primary care health system entail the involvement and contribution of ALL medical and allied health sciences schools in the country.

Leveraging Technology

51) For greater efficiency, effectiveness and economy the various components of the primary care system should be provided with computer system that links it together at least in between and among towns, provinces, and at the national level, for the collection of epidemiological data and for faster transmission of policy changes and programs in the primary health care system; this can also serve as a communication method in case of emergency conditions.

52) The Internet also allows consultations with institutions or individual doctors practicing in metropolitan areas with very special expertise by doctors in the provinces or even in far-flung areas. The age of telemedicine is here and sooner or later even some surgical procedures could be done in the. provinces, saving time and expense on the part of the patients and treatment on more timely fashion. This technology can be phased in over time. The UPCM has developed to some degree this inter-connectivity with some of

the   clinics   and   offices   in   metro   Manila.

53) In order to serve the vast majority of our people it's imperative to develop a primary care system tailored to their needs, to their financial resources and that is accessible to all, this even as we continue to build modern medical centers that cater to those with more difficult medical problems and where the problem of access due to financial constraint is not much of a factor; institution of such a high standard that will keep us in the map for medical ourism.

Access to Doctors, Question of Referral, & Consultation

54) One of the central problems of primary care system not entirely or satisfactorily resolved is whether patients should first access their primary care physician for a given medical problem, then referred to a specialist as warranted or as judged by his/her doctor, or should have the option of directly accessing a specialist if he/she chooses. Based on the presumed principle that the customer is always right, whether in fact he/she is right or wrong, the patient should have the option of seeing the doctor he/she wants to consult on a particular moment; freedom of choice is a cherished right of everyone.

55) There are positives and negatives on both sides of the issue. On the one hand, it's convenient for the patient; there are no constraints as to accessing the doctor he/she wants; there is no gatekeeper that impedes his access. Going directly to a specialist can provide a short cut to the diagnosis or treatment of his/her medical problem, which maybe complicated enough that eventually warrants referral to a specialist, anyway. The downside is that this can result in the fragmentation of care. Generally speaking, a specialist almost always focus on the problem for which a patient sees him, and usually in the context of the doctor's specialty; many times he/she doesn't have the necessary background of a patient's full past history, medications, etc., so that when he or she treats the patient, he/she may not be able to factor

some aspects of the past history and such omission may render the patient's management suboptimal or run counter to the patient's other medical problems or medicines which may or may not cause complications.

56) As I previously alluded to, the ideal situation is for the patient to first go to his/her primary care physician, then upon the discretion of his/her doctor referred to a specialist, or may request that he/she be referred to a specialist with a brief note or pertinent info why the patient is being referred. This provides a communicating tool for both doctors or health providers; and provide the doctors info as to the current problems/ medication of the patient as well as previous medical problem that may be relevant to the current one.

57) Most medical problems, say, 75% can be capably and competently handled by a good primary care doctor. And although compensation for treatment of a particular disease should be reimbursed in the same amount in theory-- a cure is a cure, or proper treatment is proper treatment--in reality generally speaking treatment by a specialist is generally more costly, thereby in the larger scheme of things, health care/medical care cost would be higher. Therefore, though the patient should have this option, this should not be encouraged, and in fact some constraint should put be in place to discourage such practices, say, by way of surcharge or co-pay. I think the PhilHealth can play a role on putting such a brake on these practices.

Hospital Care

58) There is another issue that may arise. When a patient is admitted to the hospital, who takes care of the patient?--the primary care doctor or the doctor in the hospital. There are pros and cons on both sides. In Western countries and other developed nations, the practice is that when a patient is admitted, the hospitalist, a full time employee in the hospital takes over completely in the care of the patient; when he/she recovers the patient is referred back to his /her regular doctor. In any case at the present time, this is just probably a theoretical situation; we have not yet evolved the

necessary conditions for it in the provincial/municipal setting. It should be considered from time to time or selectively depending upon certain factors or conditions

To address the question of accessibility, affordability and quality health care for the great number of our people the primary health care model is hereby proposed to be superimposed on the present health delivery system; this would have the advantage of expanding the reach of the current system without unduly disrupting it.

8
All That Jazz

Dateline: August 1, 2014

Just sharing...

For the first time I attended a jazz concert at our local library in Roseland, NJ. It was free. It was a pleasant surprise, magical.

I had never liked jazz

Truth to tell, I had had an aversion for it. Until this time But quickly, let me backtrack a bit. I think the first time I kind of warmed up to it just a tiny bit was a couple of years ago, when I happened to tune in/watch my favorite station, PBS, for Great Performances, you know, something highbrow kuno, like New York Symphony concert, an opera like Carmen. etc...all those high "cultured" programs. However, that night there was retrospective program on Art Tatum, that jazz pianist and said to be a genius of the keyboard. He was playing a piece that caught my attention. He was good, very good. After he finished, there was a brief break and it was mentioned by the narrator/interviewer that in one of his previous concerts, the legendary world famous concert pianist, Vladamir Horowitz, had to keep his audience waiting for him at Carnegie Hall for about an hour just so he can see Art Tatum's concert in another place in NYC. You can just imagine my shock. Horowitz?! Horowitz a fan of Art Tatum?! Hmm. There must something to this, I said to myself. So, I stayed with the rest of the PBS program for Art Tatum. His playing was indeed dazzling. Since then, I bought some of his records, and his playing never failed to impress me. After that I discovered Monk, another legendary jazz piano player. I was not too impressed. I have some of his records, but they remained in deep freeze. After that, my listening to jazz music remained perfunctory. Occasionally, I watched the Jazz group of Wynton Marsalis of Lincoln Center, more of forced watching, because of my positive experience with him when he was the trumpeter for the National Symphony Orchestra of Washington DC; he was superb then, I thought. But then, he abandoned classical music for jazz. I thought his shift to jazz was contrived rather than real, more of ethnic pride than true love of the music (of course, jazz music is said to be the only authentic American music and originated with or invented by Afro-Americans). So, I largely ignored him and only occasionally listened to jazz.

If you recall, I attend a piano recital of music students of NJ MTA at Montclair, NJ not too long ago.

That was a terrific experience. In fact, in many ways an eye-opener for me to Romantic music and modern "classical" pieces. I wrote about it on a previous post in this forum.

Yesterday, I went to return a book at our local library. I saw this flyer about a jazz concert at our library for free. My curiosity was picked and the memory of that concert in Montclair, NJ immediately came to mind. Hey, why not give this jazz concert a chance, I murmured to myself.

I did. And what an experience. A whole new universe, or on today's parlance, a multi-verse opened up to me.

Jazz is true music. It's not just a cacophony of sounds, with no structure, no direction, etc.

There is "method" to its "madness." It can as be cool as it can get hot, loose as it is tight, soulful and plaintive as it can be bouncy and rocking, inventive and spontaneous as far as you can take it, and still within a structure with unity and coherence. It's a musical art form as no other. In its various permutations and variations are reflected and projected the full spectrum of human emotions, perhaps even a story. It's emotive, evocative. In that it fulfills a canon of art, as the famous Filipino poet Jose Garcia Villa would have it.

To fully appreciate and enjoy it, as I previously wrote about Romantic music and modern composition, you have to fully engage your imagination and all your senses, even as the medium is mainly sound; you have to relate to it in the totality of your human senses and experience, including what is purely mental aesthetic sense.

In more experiential terms, jazz music can be seen or perceived as any other art forms. It can be seen as other human activities that enrich our lives; it can be like a fantastic basketball match between the Chicago Bulls and LA Lakers, watching the magic of Magic Johnson, and the exquisite moves of Michael Jordan, all the while being alert to what Pippin or Kobe Bryant might suddenly pull off. Or, you could be watching a movie, say, Batman, keeping an eye on the main character perform and always on the look out for a poignant counter point by his nemesis, the Joker (forgot his name; he is deceased), who steals the show.

What I noticed in the jazz playing this evening was that all the players, each of them, had the chance to show off their stuff, and while one was playing, the other guys and gals were doing their own thing in supportive role, embellishing the melodic line being played by the one on "stage, " and as if on cue, another one would take over, played for a while, while others played on the background; this pattern would be repeated many times over with the other musicians. At and at an opportune time, all played together in harmony. Somehow, the disparate segments, played by different musicians on different instruments, managed to hang together to make beautiful music. As I said, it's like watching a set play in basketball, with pass here, a pass there, a dribble down the middle, and a desperate pass made to a teammate in the right corner, the latter releasing it quickly for a basket, and the ball going in the basket with hardly a sound but a swish.

The team pull ed off beautiful buzzer-beating shot for a win. Exhilarting. You get the idea and image.

The key, I think, is to keep an open mind, be humble (i.e., admit of possibilities), be alert and let your imagination run free.

9
Beethoven, Mozart, Romantic & Post-romantic Music

Dateline: May 10, 2012 (Online Posting)

Hi Michael,

Violet and I would love to come to your concert, except there's conflict of schedule; on the same day my two apos would have their own piano recital; needless to say, we got to be there. Anyway, thanks for the invitation. Let's us know about future concerts.

Let me take this opportunity to comment on something about "classical" music. I'd like to know your take.

This past Sunday I attended the concert of Gold Cup recipients of the NJ Music Teachers' Association, Northern Chapter. There were about 10 students/recipients presented, from the youngest to two senior high students(or even first or second yr. college students). The program was heavy with Beethoven and Mozart, about 40-50%, almost juxtaposed alternatively with each other.

I listened to the pieces and performers intently and the most amazing experiences happened to me.

But before I go on, let me give you a preface. I grew up in the most unmusical family. In elementary and high school, we hardly listened to music. In high school, I might have listened to Paul Anka and Pat Boone a few times. In college, I had slept walk, never really came to know the Beatles, even Elvis; the only time I came to know Elvis was when I went to see his movie, Love Me Tender, wherein of course, he sang that beautiful love song. I knew my contemporaries went gaga with Elvis and the Beatles. I hardly cared. As I recall, the only other occasion I encountered music was when I was in college; we'd watch *Student Canteen* hosted by Leila Benitez, watching the featured "combo." Oh yes, there was the *Tawag Ng Tanghalan,* then dominated by Diomedes Maturan; I loved his signature song, Rose Tattoo. That's about it. I don't have any technical idea of what is sharp, flat, major, minor, half-note, whole-note, dah, dah. I can't carry a tune, even in the bathroom. If I sing at all, I sing to myself.

Thus, my take on music is, you might say, raw, intuitive, instinctive, unfiltered, unstudied, uninstructed, etc.

Now, this was I experienced last Sunday at the concert: Comparing Beethoven and Mozart, two of my favorite Classical composers, who wrote exquisitely beautiful music...With Beethoven one comes to know him, through his music, a "mortal man," struggling to be immortal, to soar from the ground up, breaking thru the stratosphere; his music is much like a day with overcast, with some grey clouds threatening, but knowing fully well that the sun is just hiding, and now and then, breaks through the clouds, in a burst of glorious sun rays in the full spectrum of colors and intensity. One feels at that point Beethoven has broken through his mortal struggles and is now among the gods. In a word, heroic, and you cannot help but identify with him.

With Mozart, one gets the feeling that he's, to start with, among the gods, who when they're in their best behavior, dispensing only beauty and truth to the mortals below. His music is a beautiful, cloudless, blue-sky day, with rays of the sun striking one's face, softy, gently. All seems to be at peace, no strain, conflict in the world. At night one imagines gazing into the heavens and sees only the grandeur of creation, with the firmament scintillating with myriad stars. Mozart's music engenders that feeling, at least for me. If their music (Beethoven's, Mozart's) were wine, both would be intoxicating, Mozart's is sparkling champagne, Beethoven full bodied and balanced red wine, a little sweet, a little dry.

For both composers, one sits back, listens and simply goes on with the flow...passages after passages of melodious music, and you know, you're caught up with the apprehension of beauty without even being conscious of it. It's much like, in spiritual or religious terms, contemplative experience, caught in a moment of time, nay, eternity.

At the concert, there were few Romantic pieces and modern "classical" music, aka postmodern music (where does one draw the line?), to which I had never been comfortable with...until now.

Again, I tried mindful listening in a effort to understand and appreciate it. What do you know?! I got the most exhilarating experience.

Romantic and contemporary music is lot more demanding from the listener, and I suppose, from the performer. First of all, let me tell you about my previous experience with such music. Passages seemed discordant or dissonant, many times no apparent melodic line, worse, scattered disjointed notes, such that at the end of the music one is tired, exhausted, annoyed, vexed, aggravated, rather than uplifted and relaxed. One wonders if it was worth all the effort and time spent listening to it.

That's how I had felt before. But all that changed last Sunday. And it was altogether a different experience and very pleasant one at that.

The key to listening to Romantic and contemporary "classical" music is to be fully engaged, meaning, to use your imagination and all your sense-faculties. Music, being primarily sound, therefore, audio, aural, you would normally think of only using your ear, and that's that. With Romantic and contemporary music, that would not suffice, and if you do just that, you miss a lot, can never appreciate it, only aggravated, as I used to experience.

What I did last Sunday was to engage the music with my full imagination and all my senses. For instance, for some passages in music, even as I was as listening to the sounds, I imagine scenes, visualizing forms and movements, even colors that would seem to match some notes or passages. For instance, I could imagine some sort of cat and mouse chase in some dark alley, imagine a Globe-trotters game, a car chase, a scene from ice-skating, etc...in other words, to be engaged in multi-tasking, much like what we now experience with the modern world, like texting while cooking, and heavens forbid, while driving.

I suppose the same attitude is demanded by modern art (painting). I had some intimation of this when I attended the first modern art show and seminar at Montclair Unversity,NJ at the invitation of our dear friend Teresa R., but at that time I have not yet formulated my thoughts in this manner.The same can be said, I suppose, with modern or postmodern literature (e.g. *Ilustrado* by Syjuico, which I did not particularly like when I read it; maybe I should revisit with it with the new "ATTITUDE." Who knows, I might come to like it.)

Well, I've said a mouthful. I'd welcome comments from you or from anybody.

On Thu, May 10, 2012 at 12:01 PM, Michael D.

Dear Gene,

Wow, I really enjoyed reading your letter and walking through with your thoughts about classical music. I often tell my students the words you said about imagining scenes, experiences, past or present while listening to the sounds entering into your brain. Basically, composers are like story writers, and the performers, the story tellers. Many composers who possessed wonderful gifts and amazing skills to perform like Beethoven, Mozart, Chopin, Liszt, Brahms, Bernstein, etc... are great writers and amazing story tellers. They use tonal colors, dynamics, variable pitches of sounds, rhythm and articulation of certain notes to create a language that knows no boundary or limitations. In other words, listening to music(any music) is like listening to someone speaking or telling a story.

Before I could read or write or even recognize a letter in the alphabet, I love listening to Tatay's wonderful stories. When I started reading, I look for other stories in the library written by others. I guess my point is that one does not have to be musically educated to appreciate good classical or any music and enjoy its varied complexities. All it takes is open-mindedness, imagination, and intelligence to translate the language of music as your own so it will speak into your heart with pure clarity.

As one of the greatest musician of all times, Leonard Bernstein said and I paraphrase, a word in spoken language is a note in music. A sentence is a musical phrase, many sentences connected is a paragraph. In music it is a song. Well we can go on and on until it becomes a novel or in music, we know it as a full symphonic work.

Gene, I apologize that I will do this in installment. I am preparing for our concert on Saturday. Right now, I am reviewing and re-learning more about the Bartok Viola concerto for this Saturday's concert. It is a very interesting piece which he wrote before his death. In fact he never finished it. Someone did. His materials are drawn from Hungarian folk music, Gypsy tunes and sentiments. When I heard it for the first time, I was captivated by its mysterious melodic lines and as well as its unpredictable changes in rhythm and articulation. It was quite intimidating at first and now, I embrace what he was going through in life and appreciating more of who he was as a human being. I guess, that's what you felt when you listened to Mozart and Beethoven.

I wish we could engage more on this subject but this is more fun...truly over a cup of coffee, kanin, binagoongan, sitsarong bulaklak , dinuguan and other deadly Pinoy delicacies.. We should do that.

Your Apos concert is very important. I wish I have apostolic duties now but wala pa. "nakakaingit".

I too love Elvis and the Beatles. In fact, without Elvis, I may not have started to learn the guitar.

Cheers and hope to see you all soon.
Michael

Old Wine, Late Bloom

Published by Tatay Jobo Elizes
My Book List - Contact:
job_elizes@yahoo.com - tatay@usa.com

My website - http://tinyurl.com/mj76ccq

Writings 1 Book, 2012 + + 1. Obit, *Bambi Harper* + + 2. Speech, UP, 2003, *Butch Jimenez* + + 3. Speech, Silliman U, 2006, *Butch Jimenez* + + 4. The Mission Moment, *Dr. Phil Stack* + + 5. Subanon Spirits of Rice & Land - *Noel Cornel Alegre* + + 6. I Look Out The Window - *Atty. Toto Causing* + + 7. Ride On A Bus, Poem, *Melanie Ferrer, et al* + + 8. Why Am I Doing This, *Susie Barbieri* + 9. How To Court A Philippine Lady, *Rodel Ramos, et al* + + 10. Story of Bacna Surgical Mission, *Sylvia Salvador* + + 11. Catch That Story, *Tatay Jobo Elizes*

Writings 2 Book, 2012 + + 1. There Is Hope For The Philippines, *Grace Padaca* + + 2. Pointers On Employment Abroad, *Melanie Aquino* + + 3. Without KNCHS: (Love story), *Atty. Toto Causing* + + 4. 422 Years Ago, *Rodel Rodis* + +5. Filipino American History Month, *Rodel Rodis* + + 6. A Need For Reflection, Gloom, *Cesar Torres* + + 7. Did Ninoy Die For Nothing, *Joey Concepcion* + + 8. Criteria - American Institute of Philanthropy, *Charity Guidelines (Feature)* + +9. Coming Revolution In The Ballot, *Cesar Lumba* + + 10. 2009, A Retrospective, *Cesar Lumba* + + 11. Strangers In Our Own Country, *Casiano Mayor Jr.* + + 12. The Gypsy Soul, *Casiano Mayor Jr.* + + 13. An End To Cheating, *Sonny Coloma* + + 14. Toward Culture of Giving, Not Having, *Sonny Coloma* + + 15. 100 Reasons to be Proud as Pinoys, *Anonymous*

Writings 3A Book, 2012 + +
1. EPIC25, Emerging Philippines Investors Coalition, *Norman Madrid* + + 2. Management Ability As An Issue, *Dr. Rene B. Azurin* + + 3. Do We Really Want To Give Our Politicos More Power, *Dr. Rene B. Azurin* + + 4. Will 2010 Fulfill Filipinos High Hopes For Better Life – Metamorphosis, *Ernie D. Delfin* + + 5. Comelec Is The Root Of All Evils, *Toto Causing* + + 6. Some Advantages of Federalism and Parliamentary Government For The Philippines, *Dr. Jose Abueva* + + 7. Sometimes A Great Nation, *Mar-Vic Cagurangan* + + 8. Great Conspiracy, *Mar-Vic Cagurangan* + + 9. Of Speech & Life's Riddles, *Casiano Mayor* + + 10. Bad Start To The Year, *Rod Garcia* + + 11. A Dinner out, *Rod Garcia* + + 12. One More Time, *Roy Gaane* + + 13. Strange Noises – *Tatay Jobo Elizes* + +

Writings 3B Book, 2012 + +

Eugenio A. Pulmano, MD   107

the Fighting, Clan Rules Maguindanao, *Jaileen F. Jimeno* + +XXV. Why I Publish Writings, *Tatay Jobo Elizes*

Writings 6 Book, 2010 + + I. SONA, State Of Nation Address, English, *Pres. Benigno Aquino III* + + II. SONA, State of Nation Address, Pilipino, *Pres. Benigno Aquino III* + + III. First 100 Days Speech, Pilipino, *Pres. Benigno Aquino III* + + IV. Finally, Another Ramon Magsaysay In The Making, *Bert Guiang.* + + V. A Covenant With Our President, *Tony Meloto* + + VI. From A Grateful Heart, A Thank You Letter, *Tony Meloto* + + VII. The Scent of Hope For The Global Filipino, *Tony Meloto* + + VIII. Fleshing Out The Broad Strokes, *Felicito (Tong) C. Payumo* + + IX. In Search Of Leaders (Part1), *Felicito (Tong) C. Payumo* + + X. In Search of Leaders (Part 2), *Felicito (Tong) C. Payumo* + + XI. A Conspiracy of Dunces, *Cesar Lumba* + + XII. Only Science Can Solve Poverty, *Flor Lacanilao* + + XIII. Education Reform Amid Scarcity, *Flor Lacanilao* + + XIV. Highblood: Obituaries/Reasons, *Flor Lacanilao* + + XV. How Money Works, *Edmund Lao* + XVI. State of Economy & Society, 2002, *Juan Dela Cruz (Txtmania)* + + XVII. Global Filipinos, *Juan Dela Cruz (Txtmania)* + + XVIII. Understanding Poverty, *Juan Dla Cruz (Txtmania)* + + XIX. Kuyakuy, *Dr. Ramon Marquez* + + XX. Cambodian Octopus, *Joey Jamito* + + XXI. Inspite Of Herself, I Still Love The Philippines, *Joey Jamito* + + XXII. Love Has Wings, *Percy Campoamor Cruz* + + XXIII. Walk For Kris, *Rod Garcia* + + XXIV. Coldblooded, But Alive, *Rod Garcia* + + XXV. It Takes A Village, *Rod Garcia* + + XXVI. Beauty Contest, *Rod Garcia* + + XXVII. Eight Points In Enlightening The Elites, *Orion Perez Dumdum* + + XXVIII. Case Against "Cellphone Revolution", *Sarah Raymundo*

Writings 7 Book, 2010 - My Vintage Pics (Biographical) Tatay Jobo Elizes

Writings 8 Book, 2010 + + I. The Church and the State: In Search of Common Ground, *Gel Santos Relos* + +II. President Aquino: "Walang Kaibigan, Walang Kamag-anak", *Gel Santos Relos* + + III. What Makes Us "Pinoy", *Gel Santos Relos* + + IV. Minsan May Isang Puta (2007), *Mike Portes* + + V. Build Our Dream, *Jose Ma. Montelibano* + +VI. Hope In Europe, *Tony Meloto* + + VII. Wealth in Canada, *Tony Meloto* + + VIII. Parenthood: A Sacred Covenant, *Philip S. Chua* + + IX. Are We, Humans, Really Civilize? (Or, are we for the birds.), *Philip S. Chua,* + + X. Save Our Nation, *Philip S. Chua* + + XI. A Time To Pause, *Philip S. Chua* + + XII. The Gawad Kalinga Virus, *Philip S. Chua* + + XIII. A Marching Order For P-Noy, *Philip S. Chua* + + XIV. "Bayan Ko" Bonds, *Philip S. Chua* + + XV. P-Noy's First 99 Days, *Philip S. Chua* + + XVI. The Practice of Quackery in the Phils, *Cesar D. Candari* + + XVII. Remember When? A Brief History of Old and Recent Past, *Cesar Candari* + + XVIII. The Philippines Before and What Now?, *Cesar D. Candari* + + XIX. The Traffic Problems are Beyond "Wang-Wang", *Cesar D. Candari* + + XX. Behind The Gold, *Eliseo Serina* + + XXI. May Angal? (Any Complaint?), *Greg B. Macabenta* + + XXII. Pagbalik-Tanaw Sa Kapatirang Masoneriya Sa Pilipina, *Irineo P. Goce* + + XXIII. Mysteries & Riddles Behind RP's Corridors Of Power, *Irineo P. Goce* + + XXIV. Wika - Diwa Ng Lahi, O, Ang Tore ni Babel Sa Pilipinas, *Irineo*

Old Wine, Late Bloom

Old Wine, Late Bloom

Old Wine, Late Bloom

Bayobay + + 16. Why the Philippines Need Sex Education, *Reygel Saplad Perales* + +

Timely Writings 14, 2013 + +
1The **Giant Sucking Sound and the Rise of Employnomics,** *Cesar Fernando Lumba* + + 2. **UP, College of Bus. Admin. and Cesar E.A. Virata,** *Eugenio Pulmano* + + 3. **The Missing Element in Education Reform,** *Late Sec. Jesse Robredo* + + 4. **China: Some Observations from My Recent Trip,** *Antonio Nievera* + + 5. **Don't invest in stocks if you don't have these,** *Alvin T. Tabanag* + + 6. **Creating Your Own Financial Plan,** *Alvin T. Tabanag* + + 7. **Anti-Gay Hate Crimes on the Rise in New York City: A Call to the Community,** *Kevin L. Nadal, Ph.D.* + + 8. **Native Colonialism & Subjugation,** *Anonymous (TJ Friend)* + + 9. **The Way We Were - Fond Look at a Hometown,** *Fred Natividad & Bing Castillo* + + 10. **Obituary: Common Sense,** *Anonymous* + + 11. **Be The Best Ever,** *Anonymous* + + 12. **Remembering Capt. Rene N. Jarque,** *Ellen Tordesillas* + + 13. **Why I Left the Military,** *Late Capt. Rene N. Jarque* + + 14. **Soldiers In Elections: From Pawns to Knights,** *Late Capt. Rene N. Jarque* + + 15. **Reforming The Armed Forces** - *Late Capt. Rene N. Jarque* + +

Timeless Writngs-15, May, 2014 + +
1 - **Protecting the Nation's Marine Wealth in the West Philippine Sea,** *By Supreme Court Justice Antonio T. Carpio* + + 2 – **Are Filipinos United Against China's Invasion of Ayungin Shoal,** *By Rodel Rodis* + + 3 – **Telltale Signs: Why Are There So Many Nurses in the US?** *By Rodel Rodis* + + 4 – **Telltale signs: Philippines – A Jewish Refugee from the Holocaust,** *By Rodel Rodis* + + 5 - **Telltale Signs: OFW Remittances Promote Mendicant Culture,** *By Rodel Rodis* + + 6 – **Adding Insult To Injury: UP College Named After Marcos' Prime Minbister,** *By Ted Laguatan* + + 7 - **Aquino To Nation: "This Is Your SONA."** *By President Benigno Aquino III* + + 8 – **Why We Are Poor: A Purpose for the Middle Class,** *By F. Sionil Jose* + + 9 - **Secrets of a Romantic Man,** *By Dr. Phil Stack* + + 10 - **Totoong Buhay Sa Canada,** *By Racz Kelly* + + 11 - **Small Steps to Building a Nation,** *By Bert Armada* + + 12 - **The Rising of a Nation.** *By bert Armada* + +

Timeless Writings Book – 16 , July 2014 + +
1. **The Martyrs of Camarines Norte,** *by the heirs* + + 2. **The Self-Perpetuating Elite of the Philippines,** *by Rodel Rodis* + + 3. **Isang Open Letter Tungkol sa Trapiko,** *by Ragulane* + + 4. **Truest Yet Rendered Death Ode of Rizal** by *Robert M. Bernardo, 2014* + + 5. **Aquino SONA 2014: PNoy's 5th SONA Full Transcript (English version),** *by Pres. Benigno Aquino III* .

Solo Authored Books: + + +

Book A, **Turning Points,** *Job Elizes Sr,1968 (Reissue 2009)* + + +
Book B, **Be Considerate For Once,** *Tatay Jobo Elizes (Jr), 2013*
Book C, **Piglets Unlimited - Wealth,** *Tatay Jobo Elizes, 2009* + + +
Book D, **Out of the Misty Sea We Must,** *Cesar Lumba, 2010* + + +
Book E, **Fulfilled** - *Gonzales Reynaldo, Editor, 2010* + + +

Old Wine, Late Bloom

Dook F - **Reflections** - *Bert Guiang, 2010* + + +
Book G, **Writings 7 - My Vintage Pics,** *Tatay Jobo Elizes, 2010* +
Book H, **May Bagwis Ang Pag-ibig,** *Percival C. Cruz* + + +
Book I, **Letters To Matrimony,** *Irineo P. Goce, Ka Pule2, 2011* +
Book J, **Songs I Wish You Knew,** *Soledad R. Juan, 2011* + + +

Book K, **Make My Day,** *Larry Henares Jr., 1993, Re-issue 2011* +
Book L, **Our Guerrero Family,** *Tatay Jobo Elizes, 2010* + + +
Book M, **Handy Jokes,** *Tatay J. Elizes, 2011* +
Book N, **FaveArt 1,** *Tatay Jobo Elizes, 2011* + +
Book O, **Beyond idle thoughts,** *MLMunoz, Sept,2011* + + +

Book P, **Cracks In The Armor,** *Mariano Ngan, Oct 2011* + + +
Book Q, *FaveArt 2, Tatay Jobo Elizes, 2011* + +
Book R, **Balitang Kutsero,** *Perry Diaz, Jan 2012* + + +
Book S, **FaveArt3,** *Tatay Jobo, 2011* + + +
Book T, **FaveArt4** *,2012, Tatay Jobo* + + +

Book U, **Stack Family Journals,** *Phil & Fe Stack, 2012* + + +
Book V, **Emily, An Adoption Journey,** *Romerl Elizes, 2012* + + +
Book W, **Hermes Alegre Art Gallery,** *TJ & Hermes, 2012* + + +
Book X, **Masaya Din, Malungkot Din,** *Jovelyn B. Revilla, 2012*
Book Y, **Tiis, Sipag At Tiyaga,** *Raquel Delfin Padilla, 2012* + + +

Book Z, **Until I Meet You,** *Jhackie Eslit Bayobay, 2012* + + +
Book AA, **Buhay At Pag-ibig,** *Argel Lucero Tamayo, 2012* + + +
Book AB, **Hail to the Second Best,** *Dr. Philip Stack, 2012* + + +
Book AC, **Life Bus,** *Mommy Joyce Pineda-Faulmino, 2012* + + +
Book AD, **My Candid Musings,** *Monette Dioquino Calugay, 2012* +

Book AE, **Tickets to Life,** *Maria Lourdes Jesalva, 2012* + + +
Book AF, **The Dove Files,** *Mike Portes, 2012* + + +
Book AG, **Nursing Vignettes,** *Jocelyn Cerrudo Sese, 2012* +
Book AH, **Poor Ba Us,** *R.A. Gubalane, 2012* + + +
Book AI, **Summer Idyll,** *Avelina Gil, 2012* + +

Book AJ, **Legacy (Pamana),** *Rachel Astrero, 2012* + +
Book AK, **Narratives Old & New,** *Avelina J. Gil, 2013* + +
Book AL, **Buhay Saudi,** *Adele J. Esic, 2013* + +
Book AM, **Buhay Ofw Atbp,** *Jessica Napat, 2013* + +
Book AN, **Mga Tula Ng Buhay,** *Angelita C. Esguerra, 2013* +

Book AO, **Not by Bread Alone,** *Judge Lily V. Magtolis, 2013* +
Book AP, **Jokes Collection-2,** *Tatay Jobo Elizes, 2013* + + +
Book AR, ***My Writings Sometimes,*** *Tatay Jobo Elizes, 2013*
Book AS, **Sa 'Yo Na Ako,** *Shayne A. Martinez, 2013*
Book AT, **My Kin's Family Trees,** *Tatay Jobo Elizes, 2013*

Book AU, **Rizal Family Tree & Others,** *Tatay Jobo Elizes, 2013*
Book AV, **Make My Day-2, Nice & Nasty,** *L. Henares, 2013 (1993)*
Book AW, **Make My Day-3, Cecilia, Love,** *L.Henares, 2013 (1993)*
Book AX, **Handy Lyrics-1,** *Tatay Jobo Elizes, 2013*

Eugenio A. Pulmano, MD   **113**

Book AY, **Ang Biblos,** *Rev. Dr. Eugenio Guerrero, 2014 (1929)*

Book AZ, **Make My Day-4,** *Sweet & Sour, L. Henares, 2014 (1993)*
Book BA, **Life's Journey, True Stories,** *Dr. Phil Stack, 2014*
Book BB, **Gerry Gil Writings-1,** *Danny Gil, 2014*
Book BC, **Mr. President,** *Hermie Rotea, 2014*
Book BD, **Nostalgic Pics** *1, Tatay Jobo Elizes, 2014*

Book BE, **MakeMyDay-5, Saints & Sinners,** *Henares, 2014 (1993)*
Book BF, **MakeMyDay-6, Villains & Heroes,** *Henares, 2014 (1993)*
Book BG, **Nostalgic Pics 2 (ElizesClan),** *TatayJE, 2014*
Book BH, **MakeMyDay-7, Tough & Tender,** *Henares, 2014(1993)*
Book BI, **MakeMyDay-8, Light & Shadow,** *Henares, 2014(1993)*

Book BJ, **MakeMyDay-9, Give & Take,** *Henares, 2014(1993)*
Book BK, **MakeMyDay-10, ToBeOrNotToBe,** *Henares, 2014(1993)*
Book BL, **Emily Forever In Love,** *Emily Espanol Derry, 2013*
Book BM, **The Sinatra Songbook,** *Henares, 2014*
Book BN, **The Gaborro Reader,** *Allen Gaborro, 2010*

Book BO, Ramon H. Lopez - *Art Gallery, 2014*
Book BP, **Philippines Via Old Pics-1,** *Tatay Jobo, 2014*
Book BQ, **Ronna Manansala -** *Art Gallery, 2014*
Book BR, **Philippines Via Old Pics-2,** *Tatay Jobo, 2014*
Book BS, **Being Good-A Medley Of Love,** *Dr. Phil Stack, 2014*

Book BT, **Lifestream Fisherman, A Fil.Odyssey,** *Paul Dalde, Jul2014*

Please buy online or give as gift in paperback or kindle edition. All authors and titles are easy to search, trace or find online. Thanks. Self-Publisher, Tatay Jobo Elizes

My Emails: job_elizes@yahoo.com,   tatay@usa.com

My websites: http://tinyurl.com/mj76ccq + www.jobelizes.webs.com
"Buy A Book or Gift Somebody - paperback or kindle edition online"